"By turns moving and insightful, *We Share the Sun* is the fascinating story of one of the world's greatest coaches as well as a window into rural Kenya and how the way of life has given rise to one of the most dominant sporting cultures on the planet. Patrick Sang is a man full of wisdom and compassion. It's a joy to read his story."

—Adharanand Finn, author of *Running with the Kenyans* and *The Rise of the Ultra Runners*

"'Life is like water poured on the ground. It naturally finds its course.' Patrick Sang's life journey as a humble and hard-working man who gives back is beautifully illustrated, and I highly recommend this book."

—Meb Keflezighi, four-time Olympian, New York City and Boston marathon champion, and *New York Times* bestselling author

"More than his staggering success as a coach, it's Patrick Sang's thoughtful approach to personal development—to finding each athlete's *Why*—that shines through in Gearhart's charming and deeply reported account."

—Alex Hutchinson, PhD, National Magazine Award-winning journalist, author of *Endure: Mind, Body, and the Curiously Elastic Limits of Human Performance*

"Sarah Gearhart unravels the secrets behind the coaching of the best athletes in the world. Anyone who cares about performing at your best should read this book. The stories are captivating, and the lessons are invaluable."

—Steve Magness, world-renowned performance coach and author of *The Science of Running* and *Do Hard Things*

"The great Eliud Kipchoge is a man without equal in the sport of running. Or so I thought before I read *We Share the Sun*, Sarah Gearhart's captivating biography of Kipchoge's charismatic longtime coach Patrick Sang."

—Matt Fitzgerald, author of *On Pace*, *80/20 Running*, and *Running the Dream*

"In prose as elegant as the strides of the athletes she describes, Sarah Gearhart takes us deep within the monastic world of elite Kenyan runners and their mentor Patrick Sang. Her unhurried inspection brings to life the determination, dedication, and urgency to succeed. It's a captivating study of striving at the highest level and will inspire anyone to press on no matter the challenges that confront them."

—Toni Reavis, US broadcaster, writer, and
recipient of the George Hirsch Journalism Award

"I enjoyed reading Sarah Gearhart's *We Share the Sun* about Coach Patrick Sang's leadership role in Kenyan athletics. It was interesting to learn how Sang's experiences while a scholarship college student in the US influenced him, especially the strong bond with his own coach. Gearhart reveals Coach Sang's discipline with his athletes alongside the emphasis on hard work. Runners can learn so much from this book!"

—Bill Rodgers, Olympian, four-time winner of the Boston Marathon,
four-time consecutive winner of the New York City Marathon

WE SHARE THE SUN

The Incredible Journey
of Kenya's Legendary
Running Coach Patrick Sang
and the Fastest
Runners on Earth

SARAH GEARHART

PEGASUS BOOKS
NEW YORK LONDON

WE SHARE THE SUN

Pegasus Books, Ltd.
148 West 37th Street, 13th Floor
New York, NY 10018

Copyright © 2023 by Sarah Gearhart

First Pegasus Books edition April 2023

Interior design by Maria Fernandez

The material about Wilson Kiprugut, pp. 142–144,
originally appeared in *Meter*, fall 2021.

Library of Congress Cataloging-in-Publication Data is available.

ISBN: 978-1-63936-355-1

10 9 8 7 6 5 4 3 2 1

Printed in the United States of America
Distributed by Simon & Schuster
www.pegasusbooks.com

For Ginny

Life at altitude is quiet, full of hills,

sheep scattered along the roads and children in tattered secondhand shirts, waving.

Sunshine and dry grass, hungry cattle with protruding ribs.

Fewer liters of milk as a consequence.

Auburn colored dirt coating every pair of shoes.

Plastic bottles and other recyclables that go nowhere else but on the ground.

Or burned remnants floating into the air.

Buckets of cold water and bars of soap next to a mound of clothes.

Overcrowded matatus with customers sitting on laps.

Braids. And braiders.

Varieties of mango exotic to the rest of the world.

Mosquitos, the non-malaria kind.

And runners. The serious kind.

Ones that don't run for pleasure, but for profession,

training in silence, free of headphones; no photo ops.

Somewhere, a young boy stands alone and sees this as a way to live.

CONTENTS

yote yawezekana

all is possible

INTRODUCTION

O n April 11, 2021, I sat in seat 17A, a white KN95 mask strapped around my face and wide awake at 1 A.M. en route across the world. I wondered from 41,000 feet what life would be like in Kenya as I embarked on this journey.

Due to the pandemic, domestic flights within Kenya had been suspended. That meant after flying for 15 hours from New York City to Nairobi via Kenya Airways, my only transport option to the world's mecca of distance running in the Rift Valley was to travel seven more hours with a driver who had been granted special permission by Kenya's police force.

Days later, after I adjusted to life in rural Kenya, I was relieved to sit one-on-one with Kenya's prominent running coach Patrick Sang over coffee at an outdoor patio in Iten one Thursday morning. He had just returned from Europe, where he watched his star athlete Eliud Kipchoge win the NN Mission Marathon. "I have *a lot* of questions for you," I said as we greeted by bumping elbows.

Until this moment, our discussions had been limited to a few extensive phone conversations and brief messages on WhatsApp. When we met, Mr. Sang, or "Coach" as his athletes simply referred to him, gave me his undivided attention as we navigated a four-and-a-half hour conversation about life—education, cultural suppression, trust, mental fortitude, and, of course, running, the Olympics, and coaching.

I knew even prior to our first of many meetings that Coach Sang would be insightful, someone whose words are naturally profound and are cause to ruminate. I realized very early that this book was bound to be an eye-opening and humbling experience.

This is a story about the life and journey of one of the most important figures in the world of professional sports and captures the unique and intimate relationships he has with his athletes, world champions and aspiring stars alike, for whom he serves as mentor, advisor, and life coach. Behind the scenes, Coach Sang is credited for producing some of the top professional distance runners whose extraordinary athleticism continues to raise expectations about the limits of human endurance and speed. But that description doesn't even scratch the surface of the impact Coach Sang has had on the sport of distance running and the world-beating athletes who dominate it.

Even before Coach Sang helped start Global Sports Communication training camp in 2002, he led the creation of a marathon program—the first of its kind in Kenya—that he continues to develop today. For years, Coach Sang has been carefully guiding multi-marathon winners, Olympic medalists, and record holders who have set the pace for the rest of the world's top runners. And yet Coach Sang remains mostly removed from the spotlight, unlike other prominent running coaches past and present.

While other famed coaches at the professional and collegiate levels in America have come under fire for mistreating their athletes, Coach Sang exists in contrast. His approach to coaching at his thriving program in Kenya emphasizes his relationships with his runners based on his high moral standards, modesty, and common sense. Catch just a glimpse of Coach Sang during a training session with his proteges, and it's clear that this is a man the sport needs.

The rare opportunity to spend time with Coach Sang, his support staff, and his athletes at Global Sports Communication training camp in Kaptagat gave me the impression that he is a direct, honest, witty, serious, and confident man who is simultaneously respectful and highly expectant of those he takes under his wing. I was particularly impressed by Coach Sang's demeanor with his athletes. During several training sessions, I witnessed an authoritative, humble figure who calmly spoke to his runners constructively and with encouragement, a sort of "athlete whisperer" who was stern and firm but didn't need to curse or even raise his voice. Coach Sang's gift for leadership is obvious; it's a role he's found himself in throughout his life, long before he helped build Kenya's successful marathon program, which developed the best distance runner the world has ever known. Coach Sang is a natural leader, whom his athletes deeply respect.

During much of the project, I based myself in the small town of Iten, approximately 30 miles from the camp in Kaptagat. I woke up as early as 4:30 A.M. to commute to the camp and observe training sessions. Watching these elite runners was a form of art, a gift to my eyes and mind. This kind of running is no-nonsense and serious-minded, not the recreational, do-it-for-fun type. This kind of running is for a career as opposed to a hobby. This kind of running can pull someone into a different dimension. It is a kind of running that is almost incomprehensible in its speed and power.

After training sessions, I found myself sitting next to Coach Sang and his support staff—socially distanced, of course—as he poured cup after cup of sweet creamy Kenyan tea made of fresh whole-fat milk and insisted that I enjoy it with at least one slice of thickly cut bread, baked by one of his athletes. He was a generous host, and I'm grateful to have been welcomed into his world.

By sharing Coach Sang's life and journey and illustrating how he engages with his athletes as well as how his athletes view his mentorship, I want to show readers how a good athlete becomes a great one. That, Coach Sang says, is rooted in shaping a person to have the ability to critically engage with the world with honest intention and undauntedly navigate whatever challenges life presents. What's more, though, I want readers to come away with a better understanding about Coach Sang and Kenyan running culture, particularly at the elite level. I want them to realize what's at stake when an elite Kenyan steps to the starting line at a race. Beyond the potential to earn a medal, to represent their country with pride, these athletes are running toward an opportunity for a better life, not just for themselves, but for those around them. These are runners who Patrick Sang molds into determined, devoted, and selfless champions. And, more importantly, well-rounded human beings.

PREFACE

On a 77-degree night in Barcelona in August 1992, Patrick Sang's long, slender legs trailed closely behind those of fellow Kenyan Mathew Birir* in the 3,000-meter steeplechase final. Three barriers remained.

Four years after Sang had fallen short of an Olympic medal in Seoul, South Korea, he'd earned his right to bid for one in Barcelona. And, remarkably, he'd done it on his own.

There had been no coach to guide Sang during practices at dawn in various parts of Switzerland, from Zurich to St. Moritz, where he trained on and off for several years. Sometimes, he'd have to travel for training sessions, leaving as early as 4 A.M.

There was no one to tell Sang how far to sprint or to muscle through another nauseating repetition. The final bit, that *push* is what he missed, what he would have most appreciated. A coach will test you, as will training partners.

There was no one to fist bump and commend him for his monkish work ethic, day after day. No one except for Sang. He was his own shepherd. He never questioned what he was doing. He never questioned the *Why*. The *Why* was because he wanted a medal. The *Why* was to prove he was the best of the best.

---

* Mathew with one "t," as he is quick to point out in correspondence.

The 28-year-old Sang entered the 1992 Barcelona Olympics ranked number four in the world, one year removed from his silver medal performance at the World Championships in Tokyo. Sang was favored to win the 3,000-meter steeplechase in Barcelona over Birir and their fellow countryman William Mutwol. Only after Sang had finished second at Kenya's Olympic Trials did he briefly join the two in preparation for the Summer Games. The trio had designed their own training program in the buildup to the Olympics and bonded over shared workouts in Nairobi. Though there was a coach to oversee Kenya's track and field team for the Olympics, the three men operated mostly independently of him, except for assistance with managing the stopwatch during some training sessions.

Sang, Birir, and Mutwol continued their methodical preparation during their two-week trip to Spain. They'd travel to and from the track for training absent their coach, whose attention had mostly shifted to Kenya's sprinters and middle-distance runners. Sang and Birir were not only teammates; they were also roommates in the Olympic Village. Naturally, that allowed the two competitors to eye each other closely: what the other ate, what the other drank, mirroring finite minutes of their schedules, down to the moment when their heads hit the pillow at night.

In the days leading up to the men's steeplechase final on Friday, August 7, at the Olympic Stadium, thirty-two athletes from around the world had attempted to make the cut through three qualifying heats. Only twelve made it into the final. Sang was among them, along with Birir and Mutwol. Though the three Kenyans had supported each other's efforts, all three wanted a medal. And all three wanted the gold. Only one could win.

Kenya had emerged as a global running power two decades prior, at the 1968 Mexico City Olympics, after 27-year-old Kip Keino's performance in the 1,500-meter final. He outraced American favorite and world record holder Jim Ryun. Keino had entered the Games with world records in the 3,000 and 5,000 meters, but America's Golden Boy had always defeated him with his notable explosive sprint, described as "the sting" by Charles Mukora, head coach of athletics for the Kenyan Olympic team. A native of Kenya's North Rift Valley, Keino held an advantage in Mexico City, which sits at an altitude that is upwards of 7,800 feet.

Keino opened a 20-meter gap on the American to win, despite a reported gallbladder infection that had nearly sidelined him from the race. The media praised his performance, and Keino was credited for putting Kenya athletics on the map. That same Olympics, Keino's countryman Amos Biwott raced to the top of the podium in the men's steeplechase, contributing to a trend that Kenyans would monopolize the event for years to come, earning gold in every Olympic Games from 1968 to 2016 (with the exception of 1976 and 1980, when Kenya did not participate in the Olympics).

But the country had yet to sweep the steeplechase, or any other major distance race in an Olympic final.

One of the most demanding events in track and field, the steeple-chase requires competitors to clear 28 fixed barriers positioned three feet high and also negotiate seven water jumps that are two feet deep and over an area that spans 12 feet. Agility is as necessary as endurance and speed. Without question, the steeplechase is tough. Very tough. The event requires a combination of the skills of a hurdler, a sprinter, and a long-distance runner.

At 9:05 P.M. in the Olympic Stadium, Sang, dressed in a thin red jersey sporting bib number 1138, had started in lane 6 next to Mutwol; Birir in lane 1 alongside the fastest entrant in the field at the time, Algerian Azzedine Brahmi.

The starting pistol snapped, and an assortment of powerful, sinewy legs propelled off the line in a high-speed chase. The feverish pace was problematic early in the race. A competitor had stepped on Birir's left foot, and the sharp pointy tips of his spike pierced Birir's flesh and ripped his shoe. Birir continued to run with his spike flapping, but he didn't notice blood seeping from his skin.

Two laps into the race, Birir uncharacteristically clipped a barrier and fell. Sang and Mutwol were ahead, still contending. In front of a crowd of approximately 50,000 people, Sang's lean legs spun. Birir's mind remained in the race as he quickly attempted to recalibrate. The gold seemed out of sight, but perhaps he could settle for the bronze, a surgical thought as adrenaline pumped through his body. The slimmest percentage of elites will ever have this gifted chance to file themselves in history. "You are given an opportunity. Work hard." Sang's terms for life.

By lap 4, the pain in Birir's foot slipped away. Or rather, his mind buffered the sensation. He continued his cadence until halfway into lap 6. Though Sang and Mutwol had been running mostly shoulder to shoulder, Birir crept up and surpassed both, taking the lead.

Now, it was Kenya versus Kenya versus Kenya.

Time pirouettes at an indiscernible rate when mind and body share a singular intent. Sang attempted to close the gap as he clenched his teeth and aggressively pumped his arms. *Push*, his mind repeated. The thought. The only thought. The present moment happens so fast, the mind has no mental space for anything else. Sang's 5-foot-11 frame, not a pound over 145, appeared towering behind twenty-year-old Birir, barely 5-foot-8.

Sang had long fought for this reality after he graduated from the University of Texas in three and a half years, during which he had clocked the second-fastest steeplechase time by a Kenyan prior to the 1984 Los Angeles Olympics. Unable to fly back to his home country for the Trials, he'd missed his chance to contend for a spot on Kenya's Olympic team.

But four years later, Sang earned the opportunity to compete in Seoul at the 1988 Summer Games. Though he finished far from the podium in seventh position, Sang was happy to be in the Olympics, bottom line. His driving force at that time was putting on Kenya's red, black, and green national colors. "More glory than anything else," he says.

But Sang was all the more developed for this occasion in Barcelona. Ripe. A man saturated with focus, that five-letter word tethered to purpose, the *Why*. Visibly discernible in a hypnotic stare.

Back in Sang's hometown of Kapsisiywa, in the Rift Valley of Kenya, a young boy named Eliud gathered with a few friends around a black-and-white TV. Their brown eyes widened while watching the suspense unfold late into the night as this man, known for running around the village, edged closer to first place.

Push.

Birir cleared the final barrier, his legs splashing the water before driving off the track and propelling his 138-pound frame forward. By now Birir was a few strides away from ending the story. Sang knew Birir had a better kick. The younger runner fought for his speed, gritting his teeth and glancing back twice at his countryman, eight years his senior.

Push!

A few blinks later, Birir crossed the finish line 0.71 seconds ahead of Sang, who was followed by Mutwol—and then everybody else.

The gold medal, an opportunity that Sang chased for four years, was just out of reach. Still, he was satisfied with his runner-up performance. "Silver Sang" fellow citizens would nickname him back home.

The Kenyan trio hugged at the finish line before they jogged a victory lap while hoisting the country's flag above their heads.

During the medal ceremony, the three men stood on the podium, each dressed in red track suits and delicately holding a bouquet, on display for the world to witness their clean sweep.

Their performances only added to the narrative that runners out of Kenya were outright rulers of mid- and long-distance running, and they would continue to prove to be untouchable competitors.

As fate would have it, Sang would play a role in shaping that future. But not as a runner. Under his aegis would sprout world champions, Olympians, record holders—and the greatest marathoner of all time.

kuteleza sio kuanguka

a stumble is not a fall

A LESSON IN DEFEAT

Midway through the 2020 London Marathon, Eliud Kipchoge's right ear began to plug. The Olympic champion kept his breathing steady despite pressure building inside. Kipchoge's expressionless face hid a brutal inner struggle: his 5-foot-6, 125-pound body was refusing to fight off cramps that crept into his legs, arresting his muscles up to his hips.

Unlike in years past, this historic London event was for elites only, held in a biosecure bubble shut off from the public. Due to the raging coronavirus pandemic, major marathons and local road races had all but flatlined worldwide. Athletes and support staff were permitted to travel and compete only under strict testing, travel, accommodation, and competition guidelines. Though the added measure of safety allowed the event to take place at all, the guidelines also disrupted the calculated routines of the world-class runners who had gathered to compete.

The world watched virtually as Kipchoge continuously circled the 2.15-kilometer circuit at St. James's Park in central London, anticipating him to win, true to form. Kipchoge entered the 2020 London Marathon as the fastest athlete in the field. He'd won 11 of his 12 career marathons to date[*] and was the first man to clock 26.2 miles in less than

---

[*] Kipchoge had actually completed 14 marathons before the race in London. However, two of the marathons were non-record-eligible races (Nike's Breaking2 project in 2017 as well as the INEOS 1:59 Challenge in 2019).

two hours. His four London Marathon titles and the 2:02:37 course record he set in April 2019 only added to his apparent invincibility.

The world's greatest distance runner had come a long way since his breakout 5,000-meter race at the 2003 World Championships in Paris, when he'd beaten a field of established professionals at just 18 years old, foreshadowing a decorated career. But it was in the marathon where Kipchoge found his calling when he made his debut in the distance in April 2013 in Hamburg. "I promised a course record and I did it," he reportedly said. Since then, he'd proven to be nearly unbeatable. The only marathon he didn't hang on to was Berlin in 2013, when he finished second to Kenyan Wilson Kipsang's world-record performance.

Viewers were not anticipating witnessing the most successful marathoner in history—who in January 2020 was officially named to the Kenyan Olympic team for the fourth time—lose contact with the lead pack of six men at mile 24. When Kipchoge's feet faded from his metronomic 4:30-minute mile pace, he already sensed his race was over. And it was when he crossed the finish line in 2:06:49, eighth overall and over 1 minute behind the winner, Shura Kitata of Ethiopia.

Headlines were unforgiving: "Dethroned"; "First Crack Appears in Kipchoge's Armour of Invincibility"; "Streak Comes to an End in London." It was as though Kipchoge wasn't allowed to lose. Ever. As though he wasn't allowed to be human. Ever. As though all of his successes until this race had been reduced.

"Today you are up, tomorrow you are down," the 36-year-old told a BBC reporter after the race. Kipchoge had fought through the race alone, talked to reporters alone. But he wasn't alone. Kipchoge's longtime coach Patrick Sang was there on the sideline, just as he has been since the two met in 2001.

Kipchoge grew up on a farm in Kapsisiywa, a village in Nandi County in the western highlands of Kenya. The youngest of four siblings, he was raised by a single mother, a kindergarten teacher. Kipchoge only knew his father from photos. He died before Kipchoge was born. As a youth, Kipchoge transported himself five kilometers to and from primary school on foot, often twice a day roundtrip. Later, when he was a student at Kaptel Boys High School, he developed the urge to compete. His neighbor, who lived less than a mile away, would run along the same road that Kipchoge journeyed to and from school.

That neighbor was Sang.

After the Barcelona Olympics, Sang had declined a coaching position at his alma mater, the University of Texas, and instead he moved back to Nandi to coach and also served as a member of the Youth and Sports County Executive Committee for the Ministry of Sports. He was coaching on a dirt field one day when a mild-mannered teen approached him, pitching himself as a budding athlete. He wasn't intimidated to ask Sang for a training program. They were neighbors, after all. Sang had no idea who the teen was. Kipchoge persisted, requesting a training plan. Sang went to his car in search of a pen and paper. He couldn't find either.

"Then he just got a stick," Kipchoge remembers. Sang wrote a 10-day training program on his arm. "Train for 10 days. The 11th day you rest," he instructed Kipchoge.

Kipchoge sprinted home and copied the program in a notebook.* That's when he started to catalog every workout.

Kipchoge returned two weeks later.

"What's next?"

"Who are you?" Sang asked.

"I'm Eliud."

---

* Kipchoge would go on to record every workout throughout his career. As of 2022, he has 18 notebooks.

Kipchoge's dedication was evident. He discovered early in life that "without being self-disciplined, you cannot go anywhere," he says.

Every two weeks, Kipchoge would return to Sang for a training program. And for months, Sang continued to offer workouts. He would later learn that Kipchoge's mother had been his kindergarten teacher.

As a high schooler, Kipchoge's talent for running didn't take him beyond zonal school competitions. Under Sang's tutelage, Kipchoge quickly became one of Kenya's most promising athletes, in cross country and then on the track, where he distinguished himself as a teen. Kipchoge remembers his first race in Kapsabet, 10 kilometers on the road. He won. Sang, who was standing nearby, took off his watch and handed it to Kipchoge. "I used that watch for a very long time. It was a good watch," Kipchoge says.

In 2002, barely into the sport, Kipchoge finished fifth among juniors at the International Association of Athletics Federations (IAAF) World Cross Country Championships in Ireland. A year later, during the 2003 World Championships in Paris, Kipchoge overtook world record holder Hicham El Guerrouj of Morocco to digest the victory in the 5,000 meters race. Kenya was watching him, and he knew it.

Kipchoge hunted for an Olympic medal, a bronze in 5,000 meters at the 2004 Athens Olympics; then he upgraded to silver in the same event at the Summer Games in Beijing four years later.

The narrative would shift though after he suffered a hamstring injury in 2012. It hadn't fully healed by the time he entered Kenya's Olympic Trials in Nairobi. Though Kipchoge was leading until the last 150 meters, he was outsprinted and finished seventh. Four places out of range meant he'd be omitted from what could have been his third consecutive Olympic team.

"The guy had been in almost all championships since 2003," Sang says, as though still in disbelief.

Kipchoge's mind was down.

"What do you do? What decision-making process got him there to be weighed down? Not being in the Olympics? You don't see yourself in sports anymore? Or this could have shown the beginning of your downfall?"

Perhaps the scenario of becoming a "normal" person?

It was not time though for Kipchoge to slide into retirement and assimilate into run-of-the-mill reality.

"What next?" Sang asked him as the two sat inside his house in Eldoret, contemplating a future unknown. "Eliud is like my son. The relationship between child and parent. When we talk, we talk serious business."

Kipchoge was deep in thought. Neither had the answer. Or rather *an* answer.

"Is this the end of the road? Is there anything else we can do? Can we look at running in a different perspective?" Thoughts torpedoed.

"Even if we were to think that there's life after the London Olympics, what is that kind of life? What is the picture?" Sang recalls their conversation.

Kipchoge already had medals. "What other medal is there that he didn't have?"

They volleyed critical questions and as the discussion continued, the two agreed, "Why don't we try something different?"

"Why not the marathon?" Sang asked.

Kipchoge's eyes lit up.

—⁓—

Kipchoge had never imagined he would transition to the marathon, but he was ready for a big change. For some people, the thought of running the distance of 26.2 miles can seem like a no-go zone. *Intimidating* is another way to put it. But Kipchoge points out that the way one views the journey depends on his character. "If you are talking to a pessimist, then you'll be pessimistic. But if you are talking with an optimist," he says, "that makes the mind positive." Impossible versus possible.

Even Sang admits that what Kipchoge would be capable of in the distance was a complete unknown. But as they continued their conversation, he could see that Kipchoge was internalizing what it would mean to transition to the marathon. Not just to compete, but to cement his place in the discipline. They buried the business of track. "Trying the unknown gives you a different page. You set different goals," Sang says. *Goals*, not expectations. "When you set expectations, it can really damage you mentally."

"What I've learned in life, and it started way back when I was young, is do your best. There's nothing else," Sang says.

"It was a difficult thing," Kipchoge admits of beginning the journey into the marathon, to go from high speed and shorter distances to cumbersome long runs, as he puts it. The more difficult part, he says, was in his mind. He refers to transitioning to the marathon as a trial, one in which he was excited to modify his training.

The idea of Kipchoge versus the marathon was discussed with his management, Global Sports Communication—a Netherlands-based company that represents world-class track and field and distance runners—founded by Dutchman and former elite runner Jos Hermens.

Word spread. Organizers for the London Marathon wanted the track star to headline the race, Sang recounts. What would it mean, though, to debut in a major marathon that draws some of the biggest names in the sport?

London is part of the World Marathon Majors circuit—the largest and most renowned marathons in the world, which include Tokyo, Boston, Berlin, Chicago, and New York City.

Since the first London Marathon in 1981—incepted by Olympic champion and journalist Chris Brasher and Olympic steeplechase bronze medalist John Disley—in which 22,000 people applied, the relatively flat and fast race has come to be known as record-breaking, from personal to course to world.

The marathon world record has been slashed seven times on London's course (once for men and six times for women*). The London Marathon often draws one of the most competitive fields each year, and world and Olympic champions are the norm on the start list. It has been like that for years. Appearance fees for star athletes can be upward of six figures (the *Sports Business Journal* reported that Paula Radcliffe received £250,000 to compete in the 2013 London Marathon), in addition to the $55,000 first-place prize and $25,000 for a course record.

Competitive is an understatement when describing the high-caliber, prestigious event. "London, they don't bring donkeys. They bring thoroughbred horses," Sang says, laughing.

Apart from London, organizers of the Hamburg Marathon also coveted Kipchoge and made an offer. "Our athlete agency, Global Sports Communication, had suggested Eliud to us as an athlete with great potential. We were immediately impressed by his professional attitude—this mixture of complete focus and modest manner," says Hamburg managing director Frank Thaleiser.

According to Reinald Achilles, head of communication for the Hamburg Marathon, Kipchoge traveled to Hamburg two months before the race to check out the course. "In the hotel he overheard a conversation between [the race director] Frank and our athlete manager Jurrie. Frank said it was a relative risk to put a race entirely on a debutant," Achilles recalls. "Eliud then said to Frank that when he will cross the finish line he would put on a smile for him. It was his way of saying that Frank had nothing to worry about. He [Eliud] knew that if he went to the start [line], he would win the race."

Sang remembers telling Kipchoge. "We had a two-hour discussion of the pros and cons. I put it in black and white. If you go to London and win, your name will be okay. If you go to London and finish number

---

* British runner Paula Radcliffe broke the women's marathon world record in London three times, lastly in 2003 (2:15:25). It stood for 16 years, until Kenyan Brigid Kosgei took it over at the 2019 Chicago Marathon.

four, the consequences will be too much, I explained to him, you're running against people who are seasoned marathon runners. You're coming from track. If you don't beat them, it will have a lasting impact on your mind. For you to overcome the lows, it will maybe take two or three years, which is as good as retirement."

"If you go to Hamburg, you will learn about the marathon. The competition level is not as tough as in London," Sang told Kipchoge.

"I could see he was really thinking. He was not looking at London. The offer he would have gotten was good compared to Hamburg. We never discuss money. The objective, first of all, is to focus on what they want to do and what they want to achieve." Make the cake, Sang says. Without a cake, one cannot have icing.

Kipchoge's intentions in Hamburg aligned with victory, 2:05:30, a course record by 28 seconds. He remembers feeling comfortable throughout the race, even through the last mile. A statement-making debut.

Five months later, in Berlin, he finished second to Kenyan Wilson Kipsang, who set the marathon world record in that race. What would come thereafter for Kipchoge was the building of a remarkably consistent and dominant career in the distance:

2014 Rotterdam Marathon, first (2:05)
2014 Chicago Marathon, first (2:04:11)
2015 London Marathon, first (2:04:42)
2015 Berlin Marathon, first—and he shaved his personal record to a flat 2:04

Three years after running his first marathon, Kipchoge was appointed a pre-race favorite in the marathon ahead of the 2016 Rio Olympics. The hype was real. On August 21, the last day of competition, he became only the second Kenyan to win an Olympic gold in the event, clocking 2:08:44. He finished 70 seconds ahead of Ethiopian Feyisa Lilesa.

After Kipchoge won the gold in Rio, it was becoming clearer that he was one of the finest marathon runners, perhaps ever. The world was taking notice. Nike saw an opportunity for a moon shot: offer a few of the brand's sponsored world-class distance runners the chance to collaborate to beat the two-hour barrier for the marathon. The milestone was widely thought to be unattainable. And thus Kipchoge was invited to Nike World Headquarters in Beaverton, Oregon, to discuss the proposal.

"I'm ready to explore this," Kipchoge told Sang, after returning from the trip to the US.

"As he was explaining, I was reading him," Sang said.

Kipchoge had stated to Nike that if he were to agree to the proposal, he had to stick with his coach.

"I didn't want to show any sign of doubt in me. I said, 'We'll go for it,'" Sang says. "This is a guy who is so convinced," he adds. "He took me to another level."

Dubbed "Breaking2," Nike announced the campaign in fall 2016. The quest, held on the Formula 1 race track Autodromo Nazionale in Monza, Italy, on May 6, 2017, did not go as planned. Nerves kept Kipchoge awake at 2:30 in the morning.

As part of the Breaking2 project, Nike had involved Eritrean Zersenay Tadese, the half marathon world record holder, and Ethiopian Lelisa Desisa, twice winner of the Boston Marathon. Thirty pacers were recruited to safekeep the three men. Kipchoge came the closest to achieving the sub-two-hour feat. He was on point until the last two laps, when his body detached from the target pace.

Two hours and 25 seconds later, Kipchoge finished. And while the time didn't hit the intended mark, the performance was wildly impressive, two and a half minutes faster than the marathon world record. He lived the words that Sang preaches to his athletes. "Do your best. There's nothing else."

Redemption would come in 2019.* But first, Kipchoge would break the marathon world record in Berlin in 2018.

The best competitor is yourself, Sang had told Kipchoge back in 2003. "Respect yourself, and when you are on a starting line, know that you are the best trained person. You are the best competitor of your whole self." Sang's words have always stuck with him.

This was the very champion that Sang watched unravel in London and prove that he was not, in fact, unbeatable. "The guy runs with an ear blockage, 2:06 in horrible conditions." Even on someone's best day, most marathoners will not come close to such a time, the majority of elites included.†

Sang pointed to cold rain and wind along with a missed fluid bottle as factors that impacted Kipchoge's defeat. "We went to the competition prepared," Sang assured an NBC Sports reporter. Not "he." *We.* As in Sang-Kipchoge. Kipchoge-Sang.

Disappointment hung on Kipchoge's face in place of his signature magnetic smile. "You could see he was somewhat down," says Sang, who along with a few of Kipchoge's training partners attempted to comfort him in his hotel room later that evening.

Kipchoge responded to the unforeseen loss, not dispirited, but rather with honest assessment. "Life is actually not smooth. Tomorrow there's a hiccup, up, down, straight," he says.

"I'm a believer of a philosophy of going up a tree. The tree has a lot of branches. When you step on this branch, you actually aim for the next branch. And you forget the first one because you've already stepped on it. If something happens, get the positives from it, learn from it, and move on."

---

* Kipchoge made another attempt at the sub-two-hour marathon barrier in the INEOS 1:59 Challenge in Vienna, Austria, in October 2019. He was an eight-time Abbott World Marathon Majors champion and three-time Olympic medalist by the time he took part in the highly orchestrated event.

† As of July 2022, less than 300 men in history have ever clocked Kipchoge's 2020 London Marathon finishing time of 2:06:49 or faster in a marathon.

A SILVER LINING

Not a single wrinkle traces Sang's smooth face, which appears deceptively youthful, masking a fruitful and fulfilling 57 years on earth. Maybe it's the way he smiles—genuine and so wide as though permanently fixed. Or his animated footsteps, hinting that this is a man who doesn't miss a beat. Or the way he chuckles when he shares stories about his childhood—like waiting for the school bell to ring as his signal to start sprinting from his house to the classroom. "Lazy," Sang jokes.

An Aries is described as a person with relentless determination, optimistic disposition, and a confident leader who builds community. Perhaps it was the inevitable plan that Patrick Kiprop Sang, born on April 11, 1964, would be tapped by the universe to teach others how to develop into a person with a strong moral compass who is empathetically engaged with the world, self-aware, and capable of realizing and getting the most out of their potential. This is the man Sang has become, a person with a rare gift to lead, someone who directs runners toward the best versions of themselves.

Sang grew up in Kapsisiywa, 30 miles southwest of Eldoret. Patrick with a *k* wasn't born as Patrick with a k. "My name was Patrice," he says, the name of a very close friend of his father. "I should have kept my name, actually."

Sang doesn't recall when he changed it exactly, sometime in primary school. When he was young, he thought Patrice was a mispronounced way of saying Patrick. So he altered the spelling. P-A-T-R-I-C-K. Patrick with a *k* is the name listed on his government-issued ID.

A person's second name in Kenya depends on what circumstance the child is born into. In his case, "Sang" was born outside the house. His surname "Kiprop," by the way, means that he was also born on a day "when it was raining too much."

The world does not survive without rain.

As a boy, Sang had soft hair. Most African hair has a rougher texture, "hard," he says. Rougher texture meaning tightly coiled. When Sang was in primary school, classmates had nicknamed him Warya, which, as he says, is a way of referring to a Somali. Somalian hair is softer.

The world exists in degrees of poverty and privilege. One can be poor, yet rich. One can be rich, yet poor. Where Sang came from was "a situation where sometimes you go without food," he begins. "Maybe one meal a day, and probably even that meal is not a quality meal." Poor is how he describes his upbringing. Poor as in having to go to school without certain basics and struggling to get them.

That degree of poverty is not the same as elsewhere, he continues. "Poverty in the Netherlands, poverty in the US, you cannot compare to Kenya." But not in the way we in the West might be conditioned to think. "Kenya is different. To me, being poor in the US is really being poor," Sang says. "In Kenya, somebody can sympathize with you and buy you food. People in Kenya are generous. It's from the communal way of living."

"Deep inside, when I reflect now, people that I knew then were happier than people who are considered to be above poverty level," Sang says. "I think that's another way of looking at poverty. You can have so much material things, but you can be really poor—poor in spirit, poor in social skills."

Sang says, "Development can be material, and it can be individual. You can be so developed along moral and ethical lines better than so many people, and you don't have any material things." Kenyans, he says, are privileged in ways that others around the world will not come close. "Those that visit Kenya should go home with a big lesson." He leaves the comment at that.

There is a humbleness and serenity in the Rift Valley of Kenya that seems innate, a noticeable character trait embodied in her people, from the world-class athlete to the child who runs around pushing a tire on an empty road, smiling a smile with a purity unknown to a child of the West. This child has been shielded from video games, battery-operated toys, and the latest tech gadget. This child eats food that didn't come from a package. This child wears a uniform to school, just like all his friends and classmates. There are, of course, real challenges that come with financial poverty, but this simpler, more natural life has intrinsic value that is often overlooked by those who only see what is lacking financially and materially.

The aforementioned communal way of living is another privilege. One is looked after. In villages throughout Kenya, should a child be without a parent, the child is literally raised by the village.

Sang talks little about his family. He does not wish to expose to the world the details about his siblings, his wife, or his two sons. He protects those close to him deeply. But he is intrigued about and will discuss most issues that affect the broader community around him. Ask him about politics. Education. Sexism. Racism. American history. Midwestern Vikings. His portfolio. And, of course, nerdy details about running.

Sang is a man who knows himself. Matter-of-factly, he says a lion is his totem, symbolic of leadership, fearlessness, and independence.

"I've always been myself," Sang says.

He went to church growing up. Catholic, he specifies. Even as a boy, Sang challenged his thoughts. "I was a controversial youth in church because I wanted to understand. The church had a lot of doctrines that were challenging to me. I was trying to get answers.

I'm not the type of person who follows things for the sake [of following things]."

Even as a boy, Sang looked at the world as a prism of questions and answers. Where and how he grew up shaped his way of thinking about how the world spins.

———

"It's an interesting place," Sang says of the area he was raised in. He refers to Kapsisiywa in Nandi County as "a unique community." On the surface, it looks like a small village in the countryside dotted with farms and tea plantations. But Sang speaks of that area in which both he and Kipchoge grew up with a guarded tone. "There's a lot of history behind it . . . that is not told often." Sang and Kipchoge are both Kalenjin, one of more than 40 ethnic groups in Kenya. Within the Kalenjin, they hail from a sub-tribe known as the Nandi, and within the Nandi, Sang and Kipchoge are part of the Talai clan. It is a community he describes as "an endangered species," similar to the plight of so many other Indigenous communities around the world.

The Talai are believed to be descendants from the Maasai, once the dominant tribe in Kenya that was supposedly referred to by colonial settlers as the Lords of East Africa. The Maasai, pastoral and semi-nomadic, occupied land that spanned 80,000 square miles, from Kenya's Lake Turkana to Mount Meru in Tanzania. For more than two centuries, the Maasai were ruled by spiritual leaders known as Oloibons, who held the highest place in the tribe's social hierarchy. Also referred to as a *laibon*, the position was considered exceptionally powerful: a medicine man and also a prophet to the people.

Mbatian Ole Supeet, ruler of the community for twenty-four years, was regarded as the greatest in Maasai history. His direction from 1866 to 1890 marked a period during which the Maasai experienced great unity and prosperity. It was Mbatian who had predicted white settler colonialism and supposedly had foreseen "an iron snake" that would become Kenya's railway. He warned that the community would confront an oppressive enemy and that the Maasai would lose the fight. The prophecy became a suffering truth.

The Talai, at the time rulers of Nandi, were faced with resisting the arrival of the British in the 1890s. The clan's leader, Koitalel Arap Samoei, led the opposition from 1895 until October 1905, when he was assassinated by the British chief of military intelligence, Richard Meinertzhagen. The injustices would continue.

In 1919, the British uprooted roughly 150 to 200 people of the Talai clan from their homes and forcefully herded them to Kapsisiywa—at the time a peninsula flanked by swamps and saturated with mosquitoes. They were detained to avoid resistance as the British carved space for tea plantations.

This is the part of history that gets cloudy. There's a story about Sang's family, but he knows little. For the most part he's tried to stay away from it. But his mind has remained curious. The Talai is made up of five families: Kapsogon, Kapturgat, Kapchesang, Kapmararsoi and Kapsonet. Kapsonet is Kipchoge's clan name; Sang belongs to Kapsogon. Somewhere along Sang's lineage there's a disconnect, which he has attempted to trace. "I've never heard stories about my grandfather," Sang says. To this day, he pines for the narrative of a past that is like a blank canvas, and how it may relate to the Talai clan. "Even now I don't have the answers," Sang says in reference to learning about his family's background. "I'm still trying to find out a little bit, but it looks like I've reached a dead end."

"My curiosity is that they brought families that had been branded, unwanted in the system, to that place [Kapsisiywa]," Sang says. "I don't know whether we lost the link from there or before. If there was that extended lineage, how was it? Who were these people? Were they good people, or bad people? I don't know." So many questions. The answers are somewhere Sang is delicately searching for. "I'm hoping one day," he says.

In a way, yes, Sang offers, not knowing some of his family's history makes him feel like a part of him is missing. "It's difficult to say that's a closed chapter. You can't."

Reverend James Bassey, the Talai Council of Elders chairman and Kipchoge's uncle, described Kapsisiywa as nothing more than a desolate detention camp back then. "They were herded," he says. Those dumped there were brought to die a natural death. The story has been passed down through generations. Bassey continues about the forced exodus to Kapsisiywa and its patrolled boundaries. "We were supposed to perish," he says. "God had mercy on us."

The Talai learned how to survive, attributed in part to their supreme wisdom, Bassey says. The clan had come to Kapsisiywa with their cattle, sheep, and goats, which they slaughtered for food in addition to living off of the maize, millet, and vegetables planted after they plowed the area. What was once inhabitable land slowly became acceptable, sustainable. But there is still the weight of modern history to overcome. A petition for compensation by the British and national government is still pending, in recognition of the marginalized communities that were brutally displaced.*

Those that know the Talai's deep history will describe the clan as "a very special group of Kalenjin people," says Christopher Agui, secretary of the Talai Council of Elders. "They are very intelligent. It is only resources that limit them not to advance. But when given the opportunity with resources . . ." He pauses. "Eliud is symbolic. He's our lion." Pause. "Derived from our soil." Pause. "Patrick is symbolic."

Agui continues, "If the Talai people are given an opportunity, they will do so many things."

---

* VICE World News reported in October 2022 that survivors of colonial violence and land theft have filed a case against the British government at the European Court of Human Rights and are seeking compensation of $200 billion.

They are gifted leaders, too. Successful politicians, for one. And without question, he says the Talai are blessed athletically. "The Talai have athletic talent in their blood," Bassey says.

The résumé of accomplished athletes born and bred in Kapsisiywa is extensive. Bassey scribbles a sampling on a piece of paper: Kimaru Songok, a 400-meter hurdler and among the first Kenyans to win an international medal; Amos Biwott, twice an Olympian in the 1960s who earned gold in the steeplechase at the Summer Games in Mexico City; Olympic bronze medalist Mike Boit, one of the world's best middle-distance runners in the 1970s.

Eliud Kipchoge.

Patrick Sang.

"Shrewd," Bassey says of Sang. "A no-nonsense fellow. Truthful. Responsible. Organized. A respected leader."

Sang describes his own background as "disadvantaged," a ripple effect from being born into an environment that carries such a cruel and wounded history. As a child, he wasn't aware of his lineage of suppression—at least not at first. "Gradually you start understanding your surroundings. You start familiarizing yourself with your environment," he says. "You start trying to contextualize the challenges you're going through."

"You see that there's some difference economically between your community and other communities around you. Larger land size is one way of looking at it. Earlier opportunities to get access to education. Whatever came to us as an isolated community came in bits and pieces and at a slow pace. In the end, it created a clear difference between [our community] and the rest."

Education gave Sang a window to see that it's possible to be like everybody else. In the process of going to school, he was introduced to sports—rugby, soccer, and track and field (the latter is commonly referred to as "athletics")—activities that made him feel like he had a place. "That's how human beings are supposed to develop their relationships as they grow. The foundation has to be somewhere, and for us, school was a good foundation to understand your home area, your close-knit friends."

"Those were good days," he reflects. "We even used to do decathlon. You were doing all these things not necessarily for a specific purpose. You're doing it as part of growing and as part of learning." Being an athlete was always on the side, something that complemented the core focus of going to school.

Sang started running "late," he says, at age 15. He did not grow up running miles to school. "Those are myths. Schools were placed in such a way that people could access. But the intention was not to have people run to school."

When he was a teen, he participated in his school's tradition of inter-class competition, an opportunity that came with the added incentive of an exclusive celebration for the winning class. Deciding what event to participate in was a matter of strategic guesswork. "If you were small bodied, you ran distance." One look at his lanky legs and long-limbed frame, and he was assigned to run 3,000 meters.

"I was number two," he remembers of the race, which contributed to his class winning the competition and therefore the exclusive party. The interclass competition also became a way to vet top athletes to represent the school at other competitions. "Slowly by slowly, you start valuing something. Valuation is a process. After we were selected into a school team, we were given privileges, extra milk or something. You start internalizing and start thinking, 'I have to work hard.'"

Being tapped for the school's team gave Sang the opportunity to officially train. Now, he really had a chance to present his athletic gifts, which had caught the eye of Brother Colm O'Connell, an Irish mis-sionary who would later widely become known as the "Godfather of Kenyan Running." In July 1976, Brother Colm arrived in Iten, where he taught and coached at St. Patrick's, an all-boys high school. By the time Brother Colm met Sang, his reputation for nurturing talented youth was well established.

Brother Colm himself had an unexpected path to running. At St. Patrick's, the school's cross country and track and field coach, Englishman Peter Foster, enlisted Brother Colm as the assistant athletics coach, even though his only coaching experience up until that point had been limited to soccer. A year later though, Brother Colm stepped into the leadership role when Foster moved back to England.

Brother Colm would go on to marshal a plethora of athletes that flourished internationally, including the legendary Ibrahim Hussein, the first Kenyan (and also the first African) to win the prestigious Boston Marathon in 1988. Brother Colm also guided more than two dozen athletes who developed into world champions and four Olympic gold medalists, including Mathew Birir, the man who would edge out Sang in the steeplechase final during the 1992 Barcelona Olympics.

A day in 1981 is still clear in Brother Colm's memory. He spotted a tall, lean boy racing during a meet that took place at Kamariny Stadium in Iten. That was an era when the dirt track had fresh footprints and was animated with talented young athletes who would develop into something more.

These days, Kamariny is lifeless. After Uhuru Kenyatta became president of Kenya in 2013, he had wanted to renovate a few stadiums. The legendary Kamariny Stadium—which features a public track that has seen the likes of some of the country's top middle and long distance runners for decades—was among the list. A stalled renovation has made it completely unusable. Sheep graze around mounds of soil ready for an afterlife. Those who came before the attempted renovation got to experience a more glorious era. Brother Colm is one of them. Sang, too.

Brother Colm had officiated at the meet and was impressed by how effortlessly the tall, lean boy hurdled over barriers in the steeplechase. A natural, he thought.

That boy was Sang, who would later qualify to represent the Rift Valley team at the national championships in Mombasa. Brother Colm was appointed team coach, which allowed their paths to connect more closely. When they did, Brother Colm's impression of the young Sang escalated over bits of conversation. He quickly gathered that "Patrick was a cut above your average rural schoolboy" and seemed to have a realization of what the wider world was about. He had an indefinable trait, coupled with his promising athleticism. Brother Colm earmarked him.

In 1982, after finishing his education at Kaptel Boys High School, Sang opted for two more years of advanced education at Lelmokwo High School—"A-levels," as it's known, inherited from the British system, is comparable to attending a junior college in the US. Later, Sang was offered a chance to transfer to another A-level school, St. Patrick's in Iten, but he declined the opportunity.

A-level schools were few and far between. "It was very difficult to get into one," Brother Colm says, "and to get into St. Patrick's," a school that was climbing among the best academically as well as in athletics in Kenya.

A serious and intelligent student. A serious and talented athlete, Brother Colm remembers of Sang.

What happened next was the first of what Sang calls "a convergence of destined arrangements" that have redirected his life.

"All these years from kindergarten to finishing high school, I never considered myself a sports person," Sang says.

Teaching had always inspired Sang. Teachers were the first people to be employed after Kenya gained independence from Britain in 1963. That gave him a clear picture of who succeeded through education. Sang intended to become a teacher and work toward bettering his economic situation. Leaving Kenya was not on his mind. At that time, a job was guaranteed after finishing school. The path one could follow was limited to either becoming a teacher or joining the military or the police force.

That was a different era, Sang points out. "I'm longing for a time when I was young," he says. "We lived in a [different] system in the '70s. When we were poor, everything was working. You do well in school, you get what is rightfully yours. When you apply for a job, you get a job."

Professional athlete as a career wasn't an option then like it is now. The life of athletics was viewed much differently. True, Kenyan runners experienced success in the 1960s and '70s. Olympic gold medalist Kip Keino is perhaps the most recognizable name. Success was in a different context, Sang points out. "There was no money. It was just glory. And glory takes you where in a poor country?" He continues, "The people who achieved together at the same time as Kip Keino, some of them are languishing in poverty." Amos Biwott, Kenya's first Olympic gold medalist for the steeplechase, is just one such example.

When Sang went to school, athletes were looked down on across the board. "It didn't matter if it was athletics or whatever. The turnaround came about in the '80s, when athletes started making money." More people pursued running, and then being a professional athlete began to supersede other careers, Sang explains.

During Sang's final year of high school in 1982, James Blackwood, then the assistant track and field coach at the University of Texas, navigated his way from the international airport in Nairobi to the rural town of Iten on a lone dirt road to the front of Brother Colm's door. Blackwood knew that to be successful in recruiting foreign athletes, he had to lean on someone he could trust. Brother Colm was that compass.

There sat Brother Colm at home with Blackwood, sipping tea, thinking, thinking.

"Do I or don't I? Will I or won't I introduce Patrick to Jim Blackwood?" he quietly contemplated. Sang could have an opportunity to go to college in the United States, considered "the next place to heaven" for villagers in those days, Brother Colm said.

"There's this boy at St. Patrick's," Brother Colm began. "Joseph Chelelgo. Outstanding academically. One of the most brilliant Kenyan athletes. He's in class. You can talk to Chelelgo now."

He watched Blackwood scribble in a notebook. Brother Colm's words were something like gold.

"There's this young boy . . ." The words came out. Common sense got the better of him.

"Patrick Sang." Pause. "He's a good steeplechaser. Good student. Good character. Everything," he told Blackwood. "That's the guy you want."

Blackwood continued scribbling in a notebook.

"You'll have to go to Lelmokwo to see Patrick Sang."

———

Though Blackwood had never watched Sang compete, and he didn't know any other details about him, he lassoed Brother Colm's words and drove the hour and a half from Iten to Lelmokwo in Kapsabet. Sang was in class when the headmaster called him to his office.

"I was not a troublemaker," Sang laughs, remembering the moment he was summoned. His immediate thought was that maybe something happened at home.

"This is your visitor," the headmaster said, pointing. Sang was confused. There sat a mzungu, the Swahili word often used when referring to a white person (though the term actually means wanderer).

"I'm all the way from Texas," Blackwood began in what was to Sang a nearly incomprehensible Texan accent. "I've come to give you a full scholarship." They sat and talked for awhile, long enough for Blackwood to form an impression that the young Patrick was "very pleasant" and someone he intuitively knew was worth investing in. "Other people had visited Iten for a recruiting trip. They didn't take him because they thought he had a slower time," Blackwood recalls, adding that Brother Colm had told Blackwood that Sang was "probably a 9-minute guy [in the steeplechase], which is very good at altitude."

Sang, of course, couldn't officially accept the scholarship offer without parental consent. So with permission from the headmaster, he left school and escorted Blackwood home to meet his mother.

Blackwood remembers arriving to a few huts that belonged to Sang's family. Sang's mother, who'd never gone to school, listened confusingly and curiously as Blackwood re-presented the deal: *a scholarship* to study in *America*.

"Everything is paid for," he told her. Or rather, Sang, who translated the message, told her. She only had to cover the expense of Sang's airplane ticket. The scholarship was a dream, both for parent and son.

Yes! Yes! Yes! She nodded her head and abruptly took off running, leaping over a fence in her long dress.

"Patrick, where is she going?" Blackwood asked.

Sang's mother ran excitedly to inform a neighbor of the good news. Watching her clear what Blackwood estimated was a four-foot barrier with a natural ease and grace, he immediately thought, "If Patrick can hurdle like his mom, he's going to be okay!" He still laughs at the memory.

"It was strange." Sang reflects on that moment that would change the course of his life. "When you are young, you are really idealistic. I thought that was an opportunity to experience great things." While he didn't know what was ahead of him, he didn't hesitate to accept the offer. His future life in America would cement a necessary understanding of himself and of the world.

But first, to get there the plan was to organize a harambee, a Kenyan custom meaning "all pull together." The word gained traction after Kenya became independent from Britain. The country's first president, Jomo Kenyatta, used the term in a speech. The long-standing tradition of assisting someone in need, usually led by the tribal chieftain, is primarily for a significant life event, such as an illness, funeral, educational opportunity, or a wedding.

That same year, on August 1, 1982, Kenya experienced an attempted coup. Junior air force officers took over the Eastleigh Air Base (now known as Moi Air Base) just outside of Nairobi, as well as the nearby Embakasi Air Base, in a plot to overthrow President Daniel arap Moi's government. Though the uprising failed after the government counterattacked, hundreds of people were killed, thousands were detained, and roughly $50 million worth of goods were looted, as reported by the *Washington Post*.

Sang ran at nationals in Mombasa, where he won the steeplechase event. The competition finished on the last day of July. The next day, a Sunday, the team had to travel north for a competition in Kapsabet. The route back had required the bus to pass through Nairobi, the center of the shooting during the attempted coup. The newly minted national champion sat on the bus staring out the window in the aftermath of the horrific attack.

"You cannot forget," Sang says. "Dead bodies everywhere."

The disarray was shocking. Brother Colm, who had traveled to and from the meet separately from the team, remembers being stopped by the police and commanded to get inside somewhere within 30 minutes to abide by the strict 6 P.M. curfew. He rushed to the first hotel he could find. "That whole night I could hear shooting, screaming, shouting, running."

The following morning, just prior to leaving Nairobi, he stepped outside and was ordered to hoist his arms above his head, one hand gripping his identity card.

A DIFFERENT WORLD

The crossroads: "Do I choose an academic career, or do I choose a sports career?" as Brother Colm stated.

He speaks of an era of exceptional Kenyan athletes who opted for and succeeded in both. "Patrick fits into this environment."

That is, a tier of athletes in Kenya that were recruited to American colleges in the 1970s and '80s and ultimately flourished on the world stage. One of the most prolific Western-educated talents was Nandi native Henry Rono, who was cherry-picked by Washington State in the late 1970s. Rono went on to earn three NCAA cross country titles as well as NCAA titles for steeplechase and 3,000 meters indoors. He broke world records in four distances—3,000 meters, steeplechase, 5,000 meters, and 10,000 meters—all while still a student.

One year removed from Nairobi's Starehe Boys Centre, Paul Ereng won the NCAA title for 800 meters as a freshman at the University of Virginia before he claimed a gold medal in the event (a first for Kenya) at the 1988 Olympics.

Ibrahim Hussein, a product of St. Patrick's and Brother Colm's first athlete, attended the University of New Mexico before he became the first Kenyan (and the first African) to win the New York City Marathon in 1987 followed by the Boston Marathon three times along with appearances in two Olympic Games.

And, of course, Kenya's first iconic 800-meter runner, 1972 Olympic champion Mike Boit, who graduated from Eastern New Mexico University and earned two master's degrees from Stanford followed by a PhD from the University of Oregon. The ultimate role model for people who want to bridge sports and education, "Mike is without dispute the most qualified and successful athlete-acamedition Kenya has ever produced," Brother Colm says.

At age 19, Sang was continuing the tradition when he left Kenya in 1983 to live and study in the United States, his first trip to the country. January 8—his mind specifically remembers. He flew via Sabena airline—Nairobi to New York, then to Austin—a journey that was to be alongside Blackwood's other recruit, Chelelgo from St. Patrick's. But when Sang and Chelelgo arrived in New York, Chelelgo mistakenly boarded a flight bound for Houston. Blackwood waited at the airport for the two young men and was equally as surprised as Sang when he landed without Chelelgo.

"I'll never forget seeing Patrick come down that ramp in Austin," Blackwood remembers. "He was carrying two wooden giraffes and a little bitty bag. That was all. In order to save money [by not checking a bag], he wore like three pairs of underwear, three pants, and three shirts."

College life was about to sharply contrast with all things familiar in Kenya. The dorm room. The social outings. The scrutiny of his athletic abilities.

Head coach Cleburne Price wasn't aware of the foreign talents that Blackwood had recruited from across the world. So when he initially caught sight of Sang, he interrogated him with a fury of questions:

What have you done in cross country?
I've never done cross country.
What have you run in the 1,500?
I've never run the 1,500.

What have you run in 5,000?
I've never run in 5,000.

"When I said I've only done 3,000 meters, he was disappointed because they thought they recruited a superstar," Sang remembers. "He was getting worked up. He was so furious, he told the assistant coach to organize a time trial."

"The guy was not amused with us. A time trial . . . for two people." Sang and Chelelgo. "It was crazy. To me that was an indicator that this guy is not good. Those years there was no internet. You cannot check whether somebody is telling the truth about times. It was just word of mouth."

"I was not angry. I was honest with myself, and that was the bottom line. I told myself if it's about going home, I have no problem. I've never lied to anybody. My processing was systematic and within what was right. I could have pretended that I did [all those distances]."

Sang took off on the track, his long, lanky legs elegantly yet aggressively striding across the ground ahead of Chelelgo. He ran. And ran. And ran for seven-and-a-half laps. Nine minutes and three seconds later, it was evident to the entire university track team—and to the local reporter from the *Austin American-Statesman* that Sang recalled being there—that the Kenyan's talent was no longer a question mark. While Sang's running career would soon take off, his early experience with the program left a sour taste in his mouth. "The whole process taught me a lot on how to be a human being," he says. "I was a trusting person until I went to Texas." Sang then adds, "for the first time, I felt so bitter towards another person."

Initially, Coach Price gave Sang the impression that it's okay to lie. "I think he wanted for his own ego that he recruited good athletes. I refused to buy into the process of lying," Sang says. "Up to that point, I took the Gospel to be the truth and lies were never part of my vocabulary."

"I don't blame him," Sang continues. "His job was at stake. Prior to that, there was a bad experience with some East African athletes that became nothing, and it cost a lot of money to sponsor a foreign student. So I think this guy was looking at me like, 'He's going to be another problem.'"

Sang told himself to craft his own way in Texas, at the time "a university for white people," as he puts it. "And my own way was to understand the meaning of the scholarship I got." He needed to maintain a minimum 2.0 GPA. He needed to score points for the track team. Those parameters guided how he invested his time and resources.

Sang and Chelelgo made an agreement, which included refusing to attend morning training sessions with the team. Better that they focus on their studies. They were, after all, adjusting to a new academic system. Their goal was to score points. Conference championships. NCAA championships. Score, score, score. The two met with Blackwood, who had agreed to their agenda: do well in school and earn points for the team. "In between, don't bother about the team spirit, because it means nothing to us," Sang says.

Of course, adjusting to this newly adopted life in America was a learning process, especially life in Texas. Texas was . . . different—Sang's description. "It sharpened me," he says. "The experience in Texas was part of what is necessary in life, to appreciate life and value life and find your way."

Sang learned where to show his face and where not to. In Texas "it was very clear in some communities, some neighborhoods, people like me were not allowed to go there. You could be killed." The color of his skin made his presence a question mark, as he put it. *Is he here to steal? Is he supposed to be here in the first place?*

"Jim Crow laws, separate but equal, that's what killed everything in America. Being a student of history, I could really learn things very fast," he says. "Having an open mind helps a lot. If you look at the people who are threatened, to me it is either I'm inferior, but because you're different, I have to show that I'm superior. It's a tug-of-war within a human being. Most people who express those things are suffering from an inferiority complex. They don't know themselves."

Sang briefly experimented with having a social life. He remembers the time he and Chelelgo were invited to a dinner during their first month in Texas. They went. The bill arrived. It was to be split.

"We didn't have money. We assumed we were being treated," Sang says. "Those are small things that make you really understand who you are."

After that, Sang declined social outings. Instead, he'd retreat to the library. "America taught me a lot of things. I found out that college life is different from real life in Texas. It's part of growing up, so long as you don't get lost in it."

He didn't. The guy who grew up "not a troublemaker!" was the one who could troubleshoot situations. Like the time Chelelgo was arrested. It happened when they were riding around the university on Sang's scooter.

"That scooter has a long story," he laughs. "A sign of independence. I could have bought a car. But I wanted to buy something that was practical for me." It was easier to get around the sprawling campus. Chelelgo and Sang were riding it when the university police stopped them. Chelelgo was arrested after the police found a traffic violation on his record.

Sang went back to the house he shared with a few Vietnamese students and immediately called Blackwood. Chelelgo needed bail, not only to avoid staying overnight in a cell, but also he and Sang needed to compete in a track meet the following day. Sang tried to raise money overnight, but he couldn't come up with the funds fast enough. So Chelelgo had to squander the night away until he was bailed out the next day.

"It was like a movie," Sang remembers.

A star track athlete on scholarship studying civil engineering, pulled over on a scooter and arrested. Sang's voice is animated when he recalls the details. Sang realized though how easily one can be arrested in America. Especially if they were Black.

Life there was a pile of lessons. Work hard and know yourself was his way to live. Stories unfold when he brings up his social escapades during college. Like an occasion when he was taken to a nightclub with upperclassmen. The smoking. The drinking. He didn't partake. He just watched others and realized how much that lifestyle didn't fit what he valued or wanted. "I was telling myself, this is not me. This is not my life."

He still thinks of the US fondly. "So many good things about America. If America was not a great country that gives opportunities to everybody, some of us would not have had the opportunities that we got."

Sang lived on a stipend of a couple hundred dollars a month. For extra money, Blackwood would help Sang and Chelelgo get jobs. He always looked out for them. "You have to. You can't bring somebody over that far and just, you know, get him going like that," Blackwood said. Once, during a holiday break, Sang worked in construction. A green truck pulled up. "You tell everybody that you're from East Texas," Blackwood had advised.

"We learned to stay away from certain neighborhoods," Sang says.

Sang worked 16-hour days. For one job, he rode around in a truck unloading crates of Miller Lite. "We would leave the house at 6 A.M. and arrive [back home] at night. When you arrive you don't sit down. Just go straight to the shower. Then prepare clothes for the next day. Set the alarm. When the alarm goes off, you just jump," Sang laughs. "America taught us a lot of things." Responsibility. Diligence. Hard work. "That's why I don't entertain nonsense."

Being a dishwasher at a restaurant, also exhausting and taxing, really made him think about life. "Fridays and Saturdays were the worst. On Saturdays [the restaurant] closed at maybe 2 in the morning. The buses that you were using were not there. So you have to walk home.

A lot of things go around in your head. You try to project yourself. *Is this something I can do in 10 years?* You start thinking and motivating yourself, *I have to do other things.*"

Of course, that was all on the side of his core agenda. As Sang worked toward graduating early from Texas in three and a half years, he says, the rift grew between the two Kenyans and Coach Price. But Sang says his own motives in Texas allowed him to find his way. Interestingly, in 1984, Sang remembers being the second-fastest Kenyan in the steeplechase, which more or less gave him the impression that he could have competed in the Olympics in Los Angeles, representing Kenya. But he wasn't considered for the Olympic team. Kenya's Olympic Trials were thousands of miles away back home, and it was not possible for Sang to go. Instead, he was at Hayward Field in Eugene, Oregon, competing in the NCAA Championships (he finished 4th in the steeplechase).

By the time Sang graduated in 1986 with a bachelor's degree in economics and a minor in geography, he was a three-time All-American and he set the still-standing school record for the steeplechase.

So, what was next? What was the next branch to reach for?

A friend encouraged Sang to consider graduate school—he was already enrolled in graduate courses as an undergraduate when he decided to apply. But he didn't have money to spare for tuition. Iowa State University offered Sang a scholarship. He accepted and enrolled in a master's program for city planning and regional development.

"It was like going to law school," Sang remembers. He had envisioned returning to Kenya to help build better infrastructure. "My undergraduate gave me a foundation to pursue what I really wanted, which was city planning. I came from a country that was still developing and still new. We had been independent for less than 20 years. I could see that this [education] can help me and my country when I go back."

But before Sang left Texas for Iowa, he needed to sell some of his belongings. The scooter was one of them. Blackwood uses the word *neat* when he thinks about the day he bought it from Sang for $200. "I remember driving it to my house in south Austin. I had to go down these side streets," Blackwood chuckles at the thought of awkwardly navigating around campus.

"Special," he says about Sang. "That guy was special."

By the time Sang enrolled at Iowa State in 1987, he was fully coaching himself. As part of the coveted graduate assistantship he had received, Sang administered exams to undergrads. But his professor, a sports fan, kept Sang's workload light. Sang used his extra time to train.

The university had Kenyan athletes on track scholarships, and some of whom had redshirted. Head coach Bill Bergan, who knew of Sang's success at Texas and that he had previously competed at the Drake Relays in Des Moines, asked if he would consider training a handful of the redshirted Kenyans, because they weren't allowed to officially work out with the team. For Sang, it was favorable. He could have training partners as he prepared himself for the 1987 World Championships in Rome. "It was a golden opportunity," Sang says, though he clarifies, "I was not really coaching them; I was helping them to train."

Whatever he did, the young runners followed. Sang's self-coaching experience at Texas had already prepared him well. "Self-coaching is just being aware of yourself. If you do too much, listen to your body. If you do less, listen to your body. Evaluate yourself after a competition." Sang says. "You tend to sort of mold your way into the business of coaching."

Sang did not educate himself by the book on coaching as an undergrad or grad student. He simply made up what to do after analyzing his race results, which helped him program his training (he still has a notebook with all of his workouts). Sang points to his advanced high schooling for pushing him to think critically. "The whole process of answering exams [in high school]. You have to think. Once it's in you, you also carry it to other things."

What is the difference between sleeping in a big house or a small house? Sleep is sleep, a reference he considers out loud. "This kind of dialogue within you makes you understand and develop your own perspective," he says. "That applies to running. So long as it's you who designed it. At the end of the day, you understand why you're designing it. Then when the outcome comes, you are in a position to say, 'if I had modified this a little bit, maybe I would have gotten these results.' Gradually you go into a certain direction of the system that you developed."

Sang competed unattached when he had an opportunity, a way to keep his racing sharp and vet his coaching principles. It seemed to benefit him as his abilities catapulted him onto the world stage. At the second-ever IAAF World Championships, which took place in Rome in 1987, Sang was among three Kenyans and 38 athletes in the men's 3,000-meter steeplechase. He finished eighth in the final.

Later, Sang skipped a semester at Iowa so he could focus on preparing for the 1988 Summer Olympics in Seoul, South Korea. Ultimately, he delayed his master's program for a year before he finished his degree.

—ᴍ—

"I remember in the US I talked to a guy who was a marketing person for Nike. I asked if it was possible for Nike to give me sponsorship. The guy said no. I said, 'why?' The guy said Nike does not have value in Africa. 'We don't sell in Africa. We only sell in Europe and America,'" Sang remembers being told. "This was a guy stating a fact, but he should have been a bit diplomatic. He taught me a lesson that you have to have value for somebody to recognize you."

Sang says he refused a contract worth $20,000 from Diadora, an opportunity presented in 1987 by a Dutchman who wanted to manage Sang and had negotiated with the sports brand on his behalf. "He comes with a bag of clothes and a contract. I looked at the guy and said, 'I'm not signing.' He told me, 'I've never seen a stupid person like you.' I said, 'Thank You.'"

"I said, it's not all about money. I want to participate in the process. I wish you had explained to me I'm working on something on your behalf."

So Sang closed that door and approached Adidas directly. He says the company offered to support him with training gear in addition to bonuses that were contingent on his racing success. Sang chose Adidas "because of the human way they handled me."

"Imagine a 'stupid Kenyan' refusing a contract of $20,000," he says. "That was a lot of money back then, and taking an option of bonuses. Nobody would understand. And even my friends would say, 'why?'"

He had learned from the way he was treated by the American marketer for Nike and the Dutchman; all that mattered to them was how much money he could make them, how much value his signing provided. To Sang, that was a loud message. He decided to take control, even if the terms might be less lucrative at first. The freedom was worth it. The year 1987 marked what he described as the beginning of a journey with Adidas. And over time, his decision would prove to be savvy. His Adidas sponsorship lasted for roughly a decade, until he retired from competitive running.

When Sang competed in the 1988 Olympics in Seoul, Adidas offered a bonus if he made it into the final, and even more cash if he placed among the top three. Sang said his seventh-place finish in the steeplechase final entitled him to a bonus of $3,000. He went to Adidas in the Olympic Village to collect it. "They were paying cash. They gave me an envelope. It was written with my name. I signed against it. I took the envelope. I didn't count the money. I went to my room. I opened my envelope. I had $15,000. I counted again. I counted again." He shared the news with people who were close to him. "Everybody was telling me, 'you didn't steal. You were given. Keep it.' I stayed with the money for three or four days, and I said, 'No, I have to return it.'"

He took the envelope back to Adidas in the Olympic Village. "The boss came," Sang recalls. Sang pointed out the mistake and rightfully received his share of $3,000. "I felt so good. That was $3,000 I earned, not $12,000 that I didn't."

Trust, Sang says, is something that can never be bought. He views that moment as a test of his moral position against the reality of what he was realizing could be an unprincipled world.

"I also learned about my friends—what they think about money, that money is everything. To me money is not everything. Doing what is right can take you very far."

Throughout his life, Sang has held a particular ideology. "My philosophy is that what is good will always shine. And what is right will never be tarnished," he says. "If you want to go the wrong way, you'll always see the consequences." This is a principle he tries to instill in his athletes, though he'll indirectly teach them by speaking in parables.

There's a story he tells of his youth, when his family's milk was collected and brought to a dairy processor, Kenya Cooperative Creameries. Sang remembers that a relative used to bribe whoever collected the milk. Though that relative had earned more money, his life was filled with bad luck, Sang remembers. It left a strong impression on the young Sang.

"Any evil thing you do, it will come to haunt you," he says. "Down the road I formulated a principle that I'll always try to do what's right. That's my drive. I've seen the consequences of doing right. And I've seen the consequences of what happens when you purposely do what's wrong."

"I cannot live in my conscience knowing I have done what is not right," he says.

———

During his preparation for the 1992 Barcelona Olympics, Sang was offered financial support from a Swiss running club, an opportunity he came across while traveling around Europe in 1990, after he had earned his master's degree. He appreciated that running gave him an opportunity to see the world. That included going to Switzerland to participate in a half marathon, where he met a South African woman who competed for Switzerland. "Somehow she knew me, but I didn't know her," he recalls. After the race, she asked Sang about his plan now that he had earned his graduate degree. No more schooling, at least for now.

"What's next?" she asked.

"I really don't know," he told her.

He was at a crossroads. His heart was still in running. The other option was to return to Kenya and look for a job. "I could not visualize what was ahead. I just wanted to continue running," Sang says.

She asked if he was interested in being introduced to contacts who could potentially help him advance his athletic career. "She talks to the president of a big insurance company in Switzerland, who was the president of a club that organizes a world-class meet in Zurich. The guy sends a Jaguar, and we had a five-course lunch at an exclusive restaurant," Sang remembers.

Sang was offered a proposal: he could live and train in Switzerland for six months to a year and compete for Leichtathletik Club Zürich. "Why not try," he said. So he did. Sang ran for the club from 1991 to 1998 (he is now an honorary member). He jokes he was living his life in seven-year cycles, first in the US and then in Switzerland, though on and off throughout the duration he represented the club.

"How I found myself running a half marathon in Switzerland around the right time to meet somebody," Sang says, "you don't plan those things."

But, as he has said, "Life is like water poured on the ground. It naturally finds its course."

"Switzerland gave me a serious opportunity to learn about life. I knew what I wanted to get for myself in this life," he continues. The experience, he adds, "grounded what I had crafted for myself as really critical pillars to guide me. That is, being honest to myself, being careful of the world that is really not straight. In Switzerland everything is straight. I was like Hallelujah! I'm where my value system is accepted and celebrated."

Living in Switzerland also educated him on financial matters. "When I went to Switzerland, it was a transition from being an amateur to being more or less a professional." Whatever earnings he received from his race successes were collected by the federation, Sang recalls. The athlete then had to apply to reacquire his money.

Sang would put his funds in a Credit Suisse account, eventually saving enough to qualify for a portfolio manager. "Every year I treat myself to a good holiday with my family, and it's always that account," he says. "You work so hard for what?" His goal was to have enough in the bank to send his kids to college, take care of his mother, and retire in his mid-40s.

Living in Switzerland was formative in Sang's shift from amateur rising star to dedicated professional. In Switzerland, Sang's agreement afforded him the opportunity to cover his living expenses as he trained alone ahead of Kenya's Olympic Trials. The experience of preparing for the Trials though and later for his second Olympics made Sang empathize with others like him who trained without a coach. It was a reason he got into coaching.

———

In 2000, Sang was selected to participate in a coaching program sponsored by the IAAF Regional Development Center. He studied in Nairobi, where he learned about sports science and specialized in middle and long distances. Being trained as a coach broadened his way of thinking, he says.

"When I was coaching myself, I was event-specific. You cannot do the guesswork that I was doing. It's a fact that coaching is a science. It's not emotions. It's not guesswork."

Sang finished the program in 2005 at Kenyatta University and became certified to coach within the middle- and long-distance disciplines. His coaching methods have been described as having a "holistic approach." In his mind, an athlete is not simply just an athlete. "Who are you?" is the root question he wants each person he coaches to consider. "If you take athletics out of a human being, what is left?" he says.

Most of Sang's athletes were born into a poor environment. Where you are born, the school you attend, the environment you live in deeply influences the way in which one perceives the world.

"When you are born in a poor environment, you're likely to go to poor schools. So you are likely to have limited education. When you become an athlete, this background influences how you project yourself outside and within athletics, whether you like it or not."

This background has been a common denominator among the majority of Kenya's successful runners. "[Except for] maybe one or at most two individuals, all come from rural peasant farming backgrounds. There is no athlete that you can point out that wasn't born in a rural area," Brother Colm says. "Patrick as well. He slotted into what was a very fundamental aspect of his life and lifestyle, which means young kids are very toughened in the soul. Toughened in the character. They know what hardship is about. They know what it means to suffer. They know what it means to break the pain barrier when it comes to a race. They've been through it their whole lives."

It's this kind of background, Sang says, that has driven him and his team to create a "whole-rounded person."

—*m*—

In 1995, Sang received a letter from Global Sports Communication by way of Patrick Magyar, who was the director of Weltklasse Zürich, an annual invitation-only elite track and field meet. Global Sports Communication wanted to establish a presence in Kenya. The company already had one in Ethiopia. At the same time, Sang had segued into coaching while he was a competitive athlete, overseeing a small training group that included Bernard Barmasai, who went on to break the world record in the steeplechase. The letter was a full circle moment.

While traveling in Europe in the mid-1980s, Sang's luggage was stolen on a train. He happened to cross paths with Dutchman Jos Hermens, the CEO of Global Sports (though the company was then known as Sports Communication Services). Hermens had previously introduced Nike in Europe when he worked for the brand in the mid 80s. Hermens's memory is murky as to how he and Sang connected exactly, but he remembers meeting him at a hotel. While the two weren't well acquainted, Hermens at least knew that Sang was a talented athlete. He offered Sang a bag of Nike gear, and the two went their separate ways.

A world-class runner himself, Hermens started his athletic career in his teens as a steeplechaser and later transitioned to competing in 5,000 and 10,000 meters. He was twice named to the Dutch Olympic team, first in 1972 to compete in the 5,000 meters, though he withdrew from the Munich Games following the terrorist attack on the Israeli team. At the 1976 Montreal Olympics, Hermens was a finalist for the 10,000 meters and finished 10th in a stacked field that included defending champion and world-dominating Finnish distance runner Lasse Virén. Five days later, Hermens lined up for the Olympic marathon. He finished 25th in 2:19.

Prior to the Montreal Olympics, Hermens had broken the world record for the one-hour run for the second consecutive year, and his distance of 20,944 meters (13 miles) remained unbeaten until 1991.

Ongoing issues with his Achilles tendon starting at age eighteen that he managed with cortisone injections and multiple operations for over a decade led him to end his athletic career in 1978 at age 28.

Hermens, who loved running, wanted to keep a foot in the international circuit. He thought about becoming a trainer, but at the time opportunities in the Netherlands were minimal. Hermens, alongside Brendan Foster, was the first athlete to run in Nike outside the US when Nike was only just a running company. After retiring from competition, Hermens joined Nike as a marketing and public relations manager for the Netherlands market.

In 1982, he helped set up Nike's European headquarters. He became a consultant to Nike three years later, when the European headquarters moved to the UK. In 1985, Hermens started his own company, Sports Communication Services, which later was renamed to Global Sports Communication.

Having close ties with Nike gave Hermens insight about athlete needs that could be better supported. He'd often receive questions relating to training and coaching as well as sponsorship, medical care, and general management—all issues he had during his competitive career, when he managed himself. That included arranging the competitions he'd enter.

What Hermens missed out on when he was an athlete is what he provides for those he manages, ranging from marketing to medical care. Athletes wanted to work with him. Using budget through Nike, Hermens arranged competitions, apparel, and contracts, among other things.

As a manager, the first one in the world of running at that, Hermens steered the careers of high-caliber world class athletes, like Haile Gebrselassie, a former marathon world record holder and two-time Olympic champion in 10,000 meters. Since its founding, Global Sports Communication has managed over a thousand athletes, who collectively have amassed more than 100 Olympic medals and achieved 95 world records.

Hermens wanted to set up a camp in Kenya (he had traveled to Ethiopia in 1982 and in 1985, he visited Kenya). In his eyes it was partly a way to establish a system for athletes with earnings from races. When athletes won money at a race, those around them at home wanted a piece of the prize, Hermens explained. "That's why we came to the idea of the training camp," he says. Somewhere that could have fewer distractions and would allow runners to focus and be fully supported.

How Hermens realized that Sang would be the right person for the role was an intuitive decision, he says. "I was meeting a lot of coaches, but most of them were not the right level," Hermens says. He wanted someone who could offer structure. Someone educated. Smart. Efficient. Experienced in coaching. "It was quite natural," Hermens says of nominating Sang. "Everything is in my gut feeling."

Early interactions with Sang gave Hermens the impression that here was a man that was introverted and quiet, and "deep inside, I could see he's organized, honest," Hermens says. Smart, too. "I saw the potential."

"I did not think twice," Sang remembers. He agreed to collaborate; there was, in Sang's eyes, a lack of qualified coaches in Kenya—an imbalance he wanted to correct.

The seed started in Sang's home area of Nandi County. His team rented a school that served as a training base for emerging talent. They organized time trials. Athletes who did well were then vetted through interviews.

The next step was to create a training camp in Iten. That process was bumpy as they migrated from place to place for a couple of years. "We didn't really have a clear direction where we wanted to go. That is a life I don't like," Sang says. "That's when we sat down and asked, 'What do we really want to achieve?'"

By 1999, Sang and his team aligned their objectives. They recruited a handful of men who had run at least 61 minutes in the half marathon. Once they tapped between 5 and 10 athletes, the marathon program began to develop, using funds from Nike to support the effort. Slowly they built a secluded five-acre base in Kaptagat, which officially opened as Global Sports Communication training camp in 2002.

umoja ni nguvu

strength in unity

A RESIDENCE FOR THE ELITE

The sun peeks down on a little Kalenjin boy dressed in jeans and a blue-and-white striped shirt as he marches alone on a Sedona-colored dirt road in Iten one Friday morning. His cotton shirt catches the beads of sweat gliding down his back as he lugs a 10-liter yellow jug over his right shoulder, unknowingly building his strength.

Three elite runners pass by in a phantom motion. Their presence goes unnoticed as farmers busily plow fields resembling crumbled Oreos. Cows with protruding ribs and goats tied to wooden posts strung with barbed wire stay clear of the runners' efforts. The boy, too, is unaware of the potential champions in the making as he puts the jug on the ground, finally releasing the weight off of his tiny shoulder.

Another day of life.

Iten is nicknamed the "Home of Champions." When Brother Colm arrived here in the late 1970s, the rural area was nothing more than a conglomeration of half a dozen houses, a couple of dukas (shops), and a couple of bars. No post office. No running water. No electricity. No telephone. No tarmac road.

"People never knew there was an Iten. When you mentioned Iten in the wider public, it was never seen like it is today," Brother Colm says.

That is, a mecca for world-class distance runners.

One can bank on groups as large as 60 runners (and sometimes more) meeting on a dirt path across from Tilson Timberyard as early as 6:20 A.M. The ground beneath their calloused feet is unlike any other in the world—crimson hard-packed soil that's saturated with iron and highly fertile, any local farmer will say. A bevy of vegetation grows easily. Roadsides in the Rift Valley are peppered with by-products of its dense nutrients—from potatoes and beets to carrots, kale, and cabbage.

Runners stamp this soil often twice a day, most days of the week. Evidence of their workload is hinted by dots of spit marking the ground. No energy gels are peppered on the dirt paths, or empty bottles of sports drinks. These runners also don't show up with headphones plugged into their ears. They just go out and run. *A lot.* Twenty kilometers here, 30 kilometers there. They hone their speed on softer, looser dirt at Tambach, a track that is a 20-minute ride away on a matatu (a mini bus used for public transport) for 100 shillings ($1).

Iten isn't a town for recreational runners. Here, it's serious. Here, livelihoods are at stake.

Perched above the Rift Valley's escarpment, the area has gained clout around the globe as being the world's breeding ground for distance runners. It has also become a destination for international runners. In the past, that has included British athletes like Olympic gold medalist Mo Farah as well as Olympian Paula Radcliffe, who has won seven major marathons, and members of European national teams from Germany to Denmark to Hungary. American Des Linden, the 2018 Boston Marathon champion, who also trained in Iten for six weeks, once said of its running culture, "I don't know where else you could go to find something this impressive. You can't beat it."

The town of a few thousand is part small-scale farmers and roughly a third athletes. Running is visibly ingrained here and in the vicinity. That the Rift Valley is saturated with talent only deepens the level of competitiveness. Runners like marathoner Meshack Kipkuri Kandie ("Kurui"), 30, know that. He clings to a hope of placing high enough in a race to earn money to support his family—if he can trim five minutes from his 2:15 best. Compared to others in Iten, his time is simply average.

The stakes and expectations are extraordinarily high. "What is expected of a Kenyan athlete compared to what the market expects from a German athlete? You cannot say a German athlete who is running 13:10 [for 5,000 meters] is the same as a Kenyan running 12:55. That Kenyan has to run 12:55 to be on the same level with the German running 13:10," Sang says.

"What does it do to your brain? It tells you what I do has to be better, has to be consistent so that you can continue getting the same attention," he adds. Without understanding this, Sang maintains, a Kenyan athlete can't go anywhere.

For the past decade, Kurui has supported his training with his day job as a sports masseuse, charging between 500 to 1,000 shillings (approximately $5 to $10) for an hourly session. At his busiest, he's served a half-dozen clients in a week. But the work is seasonal, as a considerable number of international athletes flock to the area mostly during the winter. Naturally, that creates an uptick of opportunity. When money is good, Kurui doesn't worry about paying his monthly rent of 2,000 shillings (the equivalent of $20). But at times he must hustle to support his wife and seven-year-old son and keep a roof over their heads. His wide smile masks the uncertainty as he slathers his hands with Milking Jelly, a lubricant resembling petroleum jelly that's used for cow udders (and is actually great for massaging runners, too).

Kurui redirects the pressure into quiet determination before sunrise, when he slips on his donated shoes and dashes off for runs as long as 30 kilometers on dirt paths full of rolling hills, where the only noise is an occasional rumble of a motorbike zipping past. This is the real work, except he doesn't get paid. He simply doesn't measure up yet, despite his ability to crank out 26.2 miles at 5:10 pace.

If Kurui resided in a major city in the US, he'd be considered elite, not fast enough to win a major marathon like New York City, but talented enough to place in the top 20 among an average of 50,000 runners. Put him in a smaller non-major marathon in the US, one that offers prize money, and he has the potential to win and earn a small source of income.

For instance, at the Cleveland Marathon in Ohio—a Boston-qualifying marathon and USA Track and Field course certified—first-place finisher Kenyan Edwin Kimaiyo clocked 2:22 in 2019 and was awarded $3,000.

At the Colfax Marathon in Denver, Colorado, the same year, of 1,500 participants, American Daniel Huben broke the tape in 2:31. Through the marathon's elite athlete program, $1,000 is awarded for a course record. The list goes on:

> **Eugene Marathon:** Winning time in 2018, 2:22 (Teklu Deneke of Ethiopia); $1,000 prize overall male
> **Green Bay Marathon:** Winning time in 2018, 2:28 (American Martin Hinze); $2,500 prize overall male
> **Indianapolis Monumental Marathon:** Winning time in 2019, 2:17 (American Nate Guthals); $1,200 prize overall male
> **Philadelphia Marathon:** Winning time in 2019, 2:16 (Diriba Degefa Yigezu of Ethiopia); $10,000 prize overall male

In the US, one doesn't have to be a top-notch elite to gain support, either in the form of a sponsorship or as an ambassador of a product. New Yorker Francisco Balagtas is an example. The 37-year-old Filipino running coach, who has completed more than 20 marathons and has clocked a personal best of 2:45, is considered a micro-influencer. He has received support from at least seven brands at one time, ranging from running shoes from Hoka, eyewear from Oakley, a GPS watch from Garmin, apparel from Ciele Athletics, and sports nutrition from

Maurten. Some of his sponsorships offer financial compensation; some support him with products.

That he lives in a major market gives him an advantage. Such aforementioned support was not handed to Balagtas. He did pitch himself to earn the partnerships. "Social media has leveraged the common person to become someone with more star power than the actual athletes with ability," Balagtas says. "While some people get their desserts, it could be taking away from others."

A less elite runner can be deemed more relatable and therefore marketable, and if they have the personality and will to take advantage of the market they're in, that can lead to a succession of opportunities. This is less possible, if at all, in a place like Iten. Local runners must get by with minimal means.

Many runners in rural Kenya who have not established their competitive credentials are self-coached and lean on each other for training tips. They wear secondhand offerings—athletic clothes that hang off their bodies in an unintentional way and running shoes donated by more economically privileged athletes, often from Europe, who visit Iten to train for a few weeks at a time; water to support a long run instead of some form of sports nutrition. In Kurui's case, black Reebok socks that cover his weathered size 8 feet, which he masks with a pair of worn out Nikes, given to him by a pro German runner. Athletes like Kurui want to build their careers. Sometimes they succeed; more often than not, they don't.

Upwards of a thousand runners are here for a singular purpose: to mold themselves into the definition of athletic success. Competition is intense on a daily basis. *Everyone wants it.*

Thirty miles away, the "Grade A" kind are watched over by Sang at a secluded training camp in an area even more remote than Iten.

—∿∿—

In 2019, the road linking Iten to Kaptagat, longer than the length of a marathon, was a wide lane of rust-colored earth. Slate tarmac has now replaced its natural state, offering an efficient path instead of alternatively passing through Eldoret. Runners continue to take advantage of the smooth, though harder, surface, apparent just before 6 A.M., when reflective piping on athletic apparel flashes in the dark, indicative of some sort of devotion toward self-improvement.

The route is mostly smooth, minus what seem like random speed bumps to interfere with the ability to maintain a lead foot. A curtain of stars above is like a faint lamp on the unlit road. Fields of maize, plump and emerald during the long rain season (March to May), but limp and ash blond when it's not (October through December), are visible as the sun begins to blush with peachy rays, gracing the day at 6:34 A.M. But before that dot of time, footprints are already evident up close as local runners in Kaptagat walk slowly on the artery of dirt that links the tarmac to Global Sports Communication training camp.

They show up much in the way that Kurui does, wanting to better themselves. For years, Sang has permitted locals in Kaptagat to attend his trainings. "Eighty percent," he estimates the runners in an average session he is simply helping. Officially, Sang coaches approximately 50 athletes; unofficially, he'll tell you the number is nearly double. Of all the athletes Sang guides, he estimates that less than 10 percent are women.

"It's never the objective to have it balanced, but it's good to have women in growing numbers," Sang says. "The problem is, if you don't address fundamental things—where they were born, where they went to school, and which type of family they were born into, top athletes fall by the wayside." Especially women. As Sang tells it, gender inequities can hinder Kenyan women from lifting themselves out of poverty through athletics. They marry and live as housewives—regardless of "whether it's enjoyable or miserable," as Sang says. "That's how we lose our women."

If an athlete finds their way to the camp's dirt track, for the most part that athlete is welcomed, so long as they have no-nonsense discipline. It helps, too, when one of Sang's athletes vouches for that local. During a typical Tuesday morning speed session, that included a hearing-impaired athlete, David Kipkogei, who lives 500 meters away from the training camp. Kipkogei says he doesn't have a manager. Since 2019, he's been showing up to train with Sang's group to improve his half marathon personal best of 64 minutes and amend his 14:28 time in 5,000 meters.

Entry into Global Sports Communication training camp is a highly coveted and testing opportunity, one that is also only a stepping stone. It is there that the real work—to the upper echelon of the sport, and also crafting a well-rounded person—begins. What makes Sang say yes to coaching an athlete isn't limited to a number they can clock; it's also what they represent as a person, or at least the potential. Sang likes to interview the athletes he'll potentially coach, to learn about their upbringing and how trusting he believes the athlete will be and find out how much he will need to invest into that athlete and how far the investment will go. "I want somebody who is going to learn. If you don't understand the sport, then I'll teach you to understand the sport," he says.

But Sang is also referring to learning about life beyond the sport. Digging into the background of an athlete is telling for how Sang will communicate with them.

"When I see them not performing, I go deeper. You cannot imagine what you find out," he says. He doesn't specify beyond the words, "A lot of complicated things." Whatever was revealed to him in confidence, Sang keeps private. "Those are small things that make me fight for these people and be hard on them. Because, you know, if you let go." He pauses. "There's a guy we trained and he became so successful. Then wrong friends took him aside. He went to zero. We tried rehabilitating him a little bit." The athlete managed to rebound, pulled himself together, and seemed as though he was back on the right track after he clocked a 2:08 marathon. Sang remembers feeling proud of the athlete, whom he doesn't name. A 2:08 marathon to him was disappointing to the athlete's manager, though. The athlete, it seemed, did not measure up after all.

Down the road, the athlete resumed drinking. "I was so mad, not at him but at the person who reversed the journey. We were traveling with this guy. I was almost giving up and said, 'No, let me wait,'" Sang says.

Later, the athlete rebounded again, apologized, and asked if Sang would coach him. He was welcomed back. "What matters is a life that has changed." Coaching to Sang is much deeper than achieving a number. It's about improving someone's life.

There have been situations in which Sang has kicked an athlete out of camp. A year trial at the elite training camp is a generous opportunity, but Sang has had to revoke it from budding talent with a stagnant or apathetic psyche. A soul drained of direction has no place in an environment exclusive to focused and dedicated professionals with lofty aspirations.

Education is high on Sang's list of keys to life success. Once, management brought Sang two boys. Sang found out the boys hadn't finished school. "Out of principle I said we cannot take school-going kids. Period. You have to finish high school," he says. He pressed the young athletes.

"Who are you?"

"What are you going to do after running?"

"Suppose you don't make it in running?"

"That's a responsible person telling you that you cannot be a professional runner without finishing school. I told them to go to school, finish, come back."

There is only one athlete who is going to school at camp and taking lessons, and that was a particular circumstance. Beyond that, everyone at camp has finished school, Sang says. "I cannot compromise my principles," he says. He points out, again and again, "The best place that gives you an opportunity to learn and watch and interact is a school setting."

"If you want to be a good professional player, you need education," he says. "Communication skills don't come from nowhere. They come from a system. One of the best systems is going to school. You don't have to be a bright student. But when you go through a school system, you develop skills—interpersonal skills, social skills, all sorts of skills." It adds to one's character.

And, Sang says, "character is everything."

Global Sports Communication training camp is situated on five acres in Kaptagat, elevation roughly 2,400 meters (7,800 feet). The land is home away from home for elites like marathon world record holder and Olympic gold medalist Kipchoge, two-time New York City Marathon titlist Geoffrey Kamworor, twice a world champion in the marathon Abel Kirui, 2017 Boston Marathon winner Geoffrey Kirui, and a slew of sub-2:06 guys like Laban Korir and Jonathan Korir (no relation).

And then there are the track stars, like Faith Kipyegon, the most dominant woman in the world for 1,500 meters. A gold medalist at the 2016 Rio Olympics, Kipyegon has won or finished as a runner-up in every major championship she has competed in since 2014. Here too is Hyvin Kiyeng, the Olympic 3,000-meter steeplechase silver medalist in Rio, who is aiming to win Kenya's first women's gold in the event.

Remarkably, this is just a sampling of the outrageous and mostly agented talent at camp. The majority of the athletes are represented under Global Sports Communication. Some athletes Sang coaches live nearby at a different camp and are represented by One4One Sports, founded by Dutchman Michel Boeting. Sang says that for those athletes who live at Global Sports Communication training camp and are not represented, the opportunity to be there becomes a recruiting tool for management.

"Just wait. Keep working hard" is a message relayed to the athletes who are not under management. Camp member Laban Korir puts it, "He can tell you there is someone coming."

Every athlete lives by the same humble standards as they wholly focus on achieving goals that are fantasy for most others in the world: A world record. Olympic title. Olympic record. A major marathon victory. Diamond League accolades.

"There were no camps like there are now," Sang says, comparing to when he was a competitive athlete. He would train in April, May, and June mostly in Zurich, some 400 meters (the equivalent of 1,300 feet) above sea level. But sometimes in the summer Sang would go to a higher altitude in St. Moritz (approximately 1,822 meters). He enjoyed it and never questioned what he was doing. "I rallied people around me to understand who I am," he says. He knew his *Why*. "Sometimes I'd have to travel to do hill work. I'd leave at 4 o'clock in the morning."

"In this profession you get your worth, your value in terms of your investment, when you get to this point. That's a change in mindset based on reality. When you have that mindset when you go there, all these things in between you don't feel it," Sang says.

"I always tell people, when I used to work in America during the school holidays, there was a time when we were working 16 hours a day. Sometimes when I see people struggling with small things, I try to reflect. How can they not do small things? It's all in the brain. I've never seen anybody working very hard and dying from hard work. They come out stronger and stronger every time they work harder," Sang says. That mentality is one he's always held close, something he tries to instill in his athletes.

Yet, it's painful to train alone, he says. "You miss the final bit, that push." The lack of a coach was another challenge. "If you are there with a coach, he can push you. Or if you have other athletes, you can recover sometimes and then they take over and you relax and push a little bit harder. Those are the things that were my challenges," Sang says.

Those things are not lacking at the training camp.

Once inside the camp's blue gate, a path leads to a small plot for visitor parking, roughly enough space for two cars. Around the corner are the athlete residences, approximately 30 rooms accessorized with two twin beds in each one—two people per room, with exceptions: Kipchoge and Kamworor each have their own rooms. One building is for men; another is designated for women.

It's cozy inside the rooms. There's enough space for a nightstand between the beds and a small table that for one athlete serves as a visible junk drawer—a couple bottles of lotion, a half dozen empty bottles (some water, some tea, Sprite), a roll of toilet paper, toothbrushes, a boxed light bulb, a bruised banana. White mosquito nets dangle from the ceiling next to a few jackets and a backpack that cling to hooks on a wall. Beds are made, offering no sign of a rushed morning after a routine wake-up call at 5:40 A.M. from a school bell on a wall in the hallway. The athletes rotate the responsibility of ringing it Monday through Saturday.

The camp is mostly run by them and has a cohesive aura. The athletes captain the ship, so to speak. There are no workers, with the exception of a cook. But even so, one athlete bakes 30 loaves of what Sang calls "the freshest bread you will ever eat" throughout the week. A high-protein mix of tight-lipped ingredients. Fluffy and substantive. No jam or honey necessary. "You won't need lunch after a couple slices," Sang says, laughing.

It's typical that athletes take turns delivering a plate of it, thickly sliced, along with a few hard-boiled eggs—"free-range," Sang says, proudly, referring to the country's Kienyeji chicken—and a thermos of warm Kenyan tea (fresh whole milk, black tea and a generous amount of sugar) to Coach and his support staff after training. They bring a few white plastic chairs to the lawn and place them in a circle, as though Sang and Co. are guests, welcome to sit after training sessions, enjoy the scenery, leisurely joke and laugh as they sip and eat.

Those who are here understand their *Why*, just like Sang understood his *Why* when he was a competitive elite athlete and trained alone.

The *Why* is crucial.

The *Why* pushes one to be better every day.

The athletes elect a president and members for committees in charge of different responsibilities, ranging from cleaning duties to managing the diet and food budget. On average, the president is not one of the top athletes at the camp, Sang says, but he notes that being a leader offers other life-changing lessons on how to strengthen themselves mentally. "The brain does something when you put somebody in a leadership position. That has been a trick for us," Sang says.

"Every time I was on a Kenyan team, I was made a captain," he says. One of the reasons Sang believes he was pushed into such roles was "to avoid problems coming from me," he says, laughing. "I gave them a lot of problems in '87, when I first came onto the Kenyan team. People were being herded like sheep, and I said, this is not the way it works." The always-on critical thinker. "When you put somebody in a position of responsibility, it changes their mindset completely."

The camp grounds are basic and stripped of simple conveniences. Inside, water-stained ceilings complement colored paint peeling away from the walls. In a bathroom with cracked tiles, a bucket is used for bathing. The extreme organization is evident, right down to blue shelves with orderly rows of dozens and dozens of running shoes, most of them free of dirt, as though they'd been scrubbed with a toothbrush and soap after training. Named after Kipchoge's friend, the late Nike Vice President of Special Projects Sandy Bodecker, there is a library with a growing number of donated books, each one stamped with a date and includes a signature from the donor; the book title, price, date donated and donor name are cataloged on sheets of paper. In the corner of the same room is a communal space with an old TV and a whiteboard that is used for weekly reading lessons. Before the camp hired a tutor, a few athletes would take turns teaching a handful of camp members who wanted to improve their literacy skills. Kipchoge was one of the teachers.

Tree tomatoes, passion fruits, banana and avocado trees, and roses dress up the landscape in the back of the kitchen and male dormitories. Meetings are usually held by the fruit trees, against the quiet backdrop.

Outside of the physiotherapy room, a cobalt-blue plastic bin, large enough to fill with 200 liters of water, is where the athletes bring their bodies for a post-training ice bath for upward of 10 minutes. They sometimes refer to it as "the freezer." They can't always take advantage of it when they want though. One late morning in early May 2021, after a grueling track session, Kaan Kigen Özbilen* wanted to calm his singed muscles after he finished eight reps of 1,600 meters. But there was no ice on offer—something that most likely wouldn't be an issue at other elite training grounds in the US or Europe, where resources aren't as limited.

Global Sports Communication training camp is far from a luxurious fortress compared to what exists in Western countries. For instance, in Flagstaff, Arizona, elevation 2,100 meters (7,000 feet), at Northern Arizona University, student-athletes and the Flagstaff community can access an Olympic 50-meter by 25-yard aquatic center; there's also an indoor 300-meter track, a 400-meter outdoor track, and modern strength and conditioning facilities along with highly specialized training equipment like the AlterG Anti-Gravity Treadmill, the cost of which ranges from $35,000 to $75,000 per model. Athletes from all over the world flocked to NAU and Flagstaff in preparation for the 2016 Rio Olympics.

Sang's runners in Kaptagat have been making their facilities work for nearly two decades without those luxuries. For a long time, there was no running water; athletes pulled from a well. That changed in 2018. "Several companies approached us. But you know, the strictness of Patrick, how he is. Before he allows you to go ahead, you have to interview first," says Sammy Sugut, a former camp resident who became

---

* Formerly known as Mike Kipruto Kigen; he changed his name to Kaan Kigen Özbilen in 2015 and officially competes for Turkey.

a member of the coaching staff in 2019. These days, the camp has piped water, but athletes still drink from the well. Now, the camp is also outfitted with solar panels for heating.

"This thing was not for elite athletes initially," Sang says. Develop something for developing athletes was the idea—on land that was a plot of forest. "We had to do serious removal. There were stumps everywhere."

Hermens, too, never imagined that Global Sports Communication training camp in Kaptagat would become what it is. He says he envisioned something even bigger. He talks about wanting to improve the camp, like the bedrooms. "It's nice, it's basic," he comments. The question is, would his vision lend the same gravitas to the nature at the heart of the facility? The athletes who come here understand that sacrifice is necessary to achieve the ultimate successes they desire. The camp's unpretentious setting has a unique ambience, sacred like some sort of energy vortex. That's what takes shape when you pull together champions and champions in the making. The mind charges with inspiration.

"It's like our office," says Geoffrey Kamworor, one of the camp's star athletes. His other home on Sundays is a large house in Eldoret, where his wife lives and takes care of their five children.

"It's not a lifetime thing you can do. Maybe the longest is 20 years," Kamworor says of his professional running career. "Of course we have a family, good houses. You sacrifice to stay away. You come to the training camp because you know what you want in life."

mwangaza mpya

a new dawn

REBUILDING A CHAMPION

The dark sky had not yet surrendered to morning as Kamworor's feet repeatedly tapped the tarmac. He was cloaked in black athletic apparel when he set out at 5:50 A.M. one Thursday morning in June 2020 to run 30 kilometers alone. The two-time New York City Marathon champion was used to training in a group in Kaptagat, but the uncertainty of the coronavirus pandemic had forced him and his teammates to disband and run solo until further notice. Kamworor was just warming up his muscles, barely a mile into the workout, when a car's front headlights flooded the road. The purr of a motorbike stalked from behind, but Kamworor didn't hear it. The motorbike driver, oblivious to Kamworor's thin silhouette, swerved to avoid the car.

In the blink of an eye, the bike knocked him to the ground. The elite runner—5-foot-7 and barely 128 pounds—lay fragile and in shock. His fingers were immediately covered with crimson red the moment he touched his head. He didn't even feel the pain in his right leg until after the motorbike driver rushed him to St. Luke's Orthopaedics and Trauma Hospital in Eldoret. Blood was everywhere. Still, Kamworor assumed the injuries were minor. But the impact proved to be more devastating—stitches to hug together two flaps of his sliced scalp as well as stitches on the inner part of his right calf, initially to pause the bleeding. An X-ray revealed a fractured tibia, which required emergency surgery to repair.

For the first time in his life, Kamworor's body was forced to pause. Sang was driving when he received the news and immediately went to the hospital.

"Athletes get injuries all the time. The one coming from an accident hits you differently," Sang says. "An accident puts you in panic mode."

Sang met Kamworor and his family in the emergency room. For many serious injuries, athletes will fly all the way to Europe for treatment. But international flights in and out of Kenya were suspended due to a nationwide lockdown. That meant the surgery would take place at the hand of a local sports surgeon. Antibiotics and pain medication helped blunt the physical suffering after the procedure to remove fractured bones from his leg. Mentally, Kamworor had to grapple with the ugly reality: One of the world's most talented distance runners would be on the road to recovery instead of attempting to qualify for Kenya's team for the Tokyo Olympics. For now.

—–—

Geoffrey Kipsang Kamworor was born November 22, 1992, in the village of Chepkorio southeast of Kaptagat, the second youngest of seven siblings raised on a farm. Commuting on foot was a natural part of his lifestyle throughout childhood; three kilometers one way from home to Chepsamo Primary School. It wasn't unusual to tally up to 12 kilometers a day.

Later, Kamworor attended Lelboinet Boys Secondary School, a public boarding school, for four years. Home was in "Kinshasa cube," named after the capital of the Democratic Republic of the Congo. All of the cubes at Lelboinet were labeled after cities in Africa. The room, shared with a dozen students, was nothing more than bare concrete walls and a lone window that spotlit aged twin-sized bunk beds layered with thin, weathered mattresses. He'd wake up, go to class, and run both in the morning and in the evening.

Kamworor's interest in running piqued after watching other athletes compete. Once he started racing, too, he became accustomed to winning a range of distances, from 800 meters to 10,000, in school and domestic events. He even won a 10K road race at age 16. Kamworor's self-confidence was still catching up. In fact, he was shy and intimidated to go to the next level and debated whether to pursue higher education. Ultimately, his racing success as a teen steered him away from his dream of becoming a lawyer, and he declined an opportunity to study at a college in the US.

A science teacher was more hopeful about Kamworor's talent. "You can run," he'd tell Kamworor. He was gifted enough to become professional—perhaps one day even compete alongside the world-class elites he'd long admired.

What came next was a whirlwind as Kamworor continued his ascension into the sport. When he was 17, he spent the summer in Europe racing 3,000 meters and 5,000 meters around Scandinavia, mostly in Finland.

Kamworor joined Global Sports Communication training camp later that year, December 2010. "Friendly," Kamworor remembers feeling when he showed up on the first of the month to meet his new training partners, which included Ugandan Stephen Kiprotich, who would go on to become Olympic champion in the marathon in 2012.

Just three weeks after moving to Kaptagat to live and train with some of the world's most talented runners, the likes of which included Kipchoge and two-time world marathon champion Abel Kirui, Kamworor claimed the under-20 title at the World Cross Country Championships, further launching him onto the international stage.

Sang didn't want to rush him into a marathon, though Kamworor had been eager for two years to test himself in the distance. The test came when Kamworor was selected as one of several pacers for the 2011 Berlin Marathon, when Olympic champion Haile Gebrselassie, one of the greatest distance runners ever, was attempting a world record alongside Kenyan Patrick Makau.

"Pacemakers are everything," Gebrselassie said. They are experienced and responsible, and manage the time while shielding the frontrunner from wind. Gebrselassie said he didn't expect Kamworor to run as well as he did—new kid on the block, after all. But after Kamworor contributed to Makau's 2:03:38 world record in that race, he proved he was ready for his turn.

And he was.

The following year, in 2012, Mark Milde, race director of the Berlin Marathon, had invited the budding distance runner to the prestigious race to run the full distance. Milde had been tracking the young Kamworor since watching him win the Berlin Half Marathon a year prior and was impressed by his diligent pacemaking in the Berlin Marathon. This time around, Kamworor would be paced by a partner from training camp, Philemon Rono.

Kamworor showed up at Tegel Airport in Berlin dressed in a white ball cap, a leatherish brown jacket over a maroon shirt, and pants that hung on his lean frame. He smiled gently as he wheeled around a carry-on suitcase. Time would pass at the athlete hotel; when he wasn't attending technical meetings, he was quietly lounging on his bed.

The morning of the race, which was to begin at 9 A.M., Kamworor was instructed to eat breakfast at 6 A.M. He made way to the starting line dressed in a black Nike tracksuit. "No pressure." The two words he spoke out loud before the race, captured on camera by Dutch filmmaker Boudewijn de Kemp, who followed the journey in the documentary *The Unknown Runner.*

Kamworor stood behind a few pacers, his tracksuit delayered, revealing well-crafted legs that had experienced too many kilometers. A pacer helped double knot Kamworor's orange Nikes. As the elites were called to the starting line, the man designated as bib number 20 on his back and "Kipsang" on the front made way to meet whatever fate had in store.

Nearly 40,000 runners stood behind him as he bounced up and down alongside Kenyan Dennis Kimetto, not yet the world record holder, but one in the making. Whether he was shaking off nerves relating to the unknown territory Kamworor was set to embark on or simply a means to warm his body, only he knows that truth.

Kamworor, who chased from the sound of the starting pistol, was broadcasted as "the one with the grayish top, in the middle," a contender to pay attention to, and further described as a mature youngster.

He was part of the pack with Kimetto, Geoffrey Mutai, and Jonathan Maiyo—Kenya times four. "Who will be brave enough?" a sportscaster asked, after the group had surpassed 30 kilometers (of 42.1 total). Mutai and Kimetto, the two training partners, broke off. Kamworor hung on in third place.

The great coincidence was that he would be debuting in the marathon on the same course where he'd led one of the sport's most renowned legends, Gebrselassie. Kamworor had prepared for this day with extra hill training, including on Sundays, the sacred day off typically reserved for church, spending with family, and personal time.

"Desperately" hanging on, "desperately" trying to stay in—the announcer used that word twice. Kamworor sprinted through Brandenburg Gate and down the homestretch. Alone. And yet not. Fans flanked both sidelines and erupted with cheers and claps as Kamworor approached the finish, nearly ending his journey in no-man's-land.

He was just 19 years old when his feet crossed the finish line in 2:06:12, third overall behind 28-year-old Kimetto and the winner, 31-year-old Mutai.

But Kamworor was expecting to run 2:05. For the underdog, it's okay to run a minute off your intended mark. It's okay to lose.

Except for him, it really wasn't.

"2:06 is not bad," he said quietly, seemingly half convinced. "I'm not hurt about it."

Sang describes Kamworor as one of the few exceptional athletes he's ever encountered in his career driven by something that at the time Sang couldn't quite figure out. Just like Brother Colm saw something in Sang. "You get a feeling about something. You say, I'm not sure, but we'll find out together what is there," Brother Colm says.

Kamworor is what Sang would describe as "the real wheat," what's left after the husk and impurities like dirt and stones are removed. The grain is what you want.

—∿∿—

Life at camp is free from distractions. Tame. Quiet. Peaceful. The opposite of life outside of the bubble when an infectious respiratory disease began to occupy the world.

The first case of the coronavirus in Kenya was confirmed on March 12, 2020, when a 27-year-old Kenyan woman tested positive after she landed in Nairobi upon returning from the US via London. Three days later, Kenya's president Uhuru Kenyatta issued an aggressive executive order that included a partial lockdown across the country to manage the transmission of the coronavirus. Schools were shuttered, incoming international flights were suspended, and other sweeping travel restrictions were issued. With the exception of essential service people, residents were ordered to work from home. Health cabinet secretary Mutahi Kagwe banned all social gatherings. A nationwide curfew was ordered from 7 P.M. to 5 A.M., effective March 27, 2020. The Ministry of Sports, Culture, and Heritage called for a cessation of sports competitions and group sports activities.

For the safety of himself, his staff, and the athletes, Sang had no choice but to close the training camp and send everyone home. He offered workouts and tracked progress through WhatsApp. No more shared track sessions; group long runs at dawn were replaced with solo efforts on lifeless roads. Staying healthy became the priority, as in shielding themselves from the mysterious "monster that landed" as Sang put it.

Wycliffe Kinyamal, an 800-meter specialist who joined the camp in 2017, was the lone athlete Sang permitted to remain on the grounds. Kinyamal, part of the Maasai tribe, grew up 11 kilometers from two-time Olympic champion David Rudisha in Narok County next to the Maasai Mara National Reserve, approximately 150 kilometers south of Kaptagat. The area is not quite as conducive for training, Kinyamal says. Running professionally is less of a norm, and the terrain pales in comparison to the dirt trails around Kaptagat, which sits at a higher altitude compared to his hometown.

As opportunities to race on the international and domestic circuits dissolved, Kinyamal still felt like he was on call. An elite runner can't exactly suddenly neglect his profession. His speed. His endurance. His strength. The three aspects of training that Sang says need to be balanced when building an athlete. The way Kinyamal saw it, he should keep himself charged *if* and *when* he might travel for the Diamond League meets, a series of the best invitational track and field competitions around the world.

So Kinyamal lived alone at camp, for months. He'd listen to traditional Maasai music to cut the silence. Instead of the camp's cook there to prepare bowls of teff porridge, batches of ugali, thermoses of Kenyan tea, and stacks of soft, flaky chapati, Kinyamal made every meal himself. He trained on vacant roads around Kaptagat, occasionally joining another athlete in the area for a session. He watched as the plot of land next to the camp's guest parking area transformed into a dirt track. Construction for it got underway in March 2020. Previously, the team would travel to Eldoret to train on a track at Moi University.

Little did Sang know that closing camp was only the start of the challenges that lay ahead.

The world didn't know what it didn't know when the coronavirus was first introduced in late December 2019 in Wuhan, China.

By January 2020, World Health Organization director-general Dr. Tedros Adhanom Ghebreyesus declared a public health emergency, one of international concern, the highest level of alarm. Fever, coughing, chills, and loss of smell and taste were common symptoms. Difficulty breathing, shortness of breath, and chest pain were among the more serious identifiable signs of the virus.

By the end of January, Italy had become the epicenter. The government's army was sent to the northern region to enforce the nationwide lockdown. Prime Minister Giuseppe Conte described the situation as the most difficult crisis since World War II. It was a disturbing sign of what was to come. Shutdowns ensued—around Europe, the United States, and the world.

As the coronavirus spread around the globe, survival became everyone's priority. In various corners, "survival" led to a mad rush to stockpile toilet paper and other items in bulk. "That tells you what goes on in the mind of a human being," Sang says.

Total confusion.

By mid-May 2020, Kenya had tallied more than 1,000 cases of the coronavirus. Weeks after the lockdown was announced, at the direction of President Kenyatta, the Ministry of Sports set aside 100 million shillings (roughly $820,000) from the Sports, Arts, and Social Development Fund to support athletes coping with the dire effects of the pandemic, like the loss of potential income due to a complete absence of racing opportunities.

In Kenya, particularly in the Rift Valley, there are many runners and few competitions that pay. "It pushes things to the way Darwin thought many years back," Sang once told a filmmaker. "The survival of the fittest."

The difference between a race in Kenya and a race in Europe or the US is striking to witness in person. In Kenya, it's not unusual for a couple hundred elites to show up, Sang points out, whereas elsewhere the percentage of elites is significantly smaller. In Kenya, people run less for leisure and fun. "They come into the sport to make a living," he says. That is the driving force: to fight poverty.

Kipchoge had told Kenya's independent newspaper, *The Daily Nation*, that up to 80 percent of athletes depend on international races. He pointed out that more than 2,000 active athletes in Kenya were in need of aid during the pandemic. Retired athletes, too. The National Olympic Committee of Kenya had targeted former athletes, like Paralympian and 1,500-meter gold medalist Abraham Tarbei, to benefit from assistance.

The Ministry of Sports had named Kipchoge an ambassador for a food relief project. One Friday in May 2020, Kipchoge could be seen in a red Nike shirt, black pants, and a KN95 mask lugging a cardboard box of supplies that included wheat flour, maize flour, and cooking oil, donated by the ministry and the Hindu Council of Kenya. He helped distribute supplies to nearly 70 athletes. He visited three counties in half a day, toting the items in his Isuzu D-Max. Kipchoge also collaborated with Eldoret Grains Limited to supply food.

A dozen athletes here, five dozen athletes there, another two dozen, then a few more dozen. Sweaters in addition to food. Blankets. A solar power kit. Sanitary pads. One week. Two weeks. Three weeks. April. May. June. And beyond. In Kericho County. Kapsabet. Eldoret. Iten.

And "in the process of distributing food, somebody collapsed," Sang remembers witnessing during a relief trip with Kipchoge in Iten, one of three they made together to the area at the onset of the pandemic. "That is the background I want to put in the picture. The real picture," Sang says.

"There was an Indian athlete that had no food. It was a big story in the paper the next day. They took a picture of him getting food from Eliud. The next thing, the Indian community in the country, I think they panicked. Many were calling, wanting to give things to the [Eliud Kipchoge] Foundation. It was unique to see."

"Everything will be okay," Iten resident Ben Kiplagat remembers hearing Kipchoge tell runners like himself when he retrieved a box of supplies allocated at a local primary school.

"We are in this together," Kipchoge would say.

As the world struggled to bring the pandemic under control, everything about everything remained uncertain, the sporting calendar in particular. The summer of 2020 was to be a global date with the Tokyo Olympics. The opening ceremony was planned for July 24. Finally, after four years of waiting, the crème de la crème of 33 different sports and from more than 200 countries would gather to participate in the Games in the spirit of solidarity, friendship and fair play.

Would Kipchoge defend his marathon title? Would Kipyegon repeat her 1,500-meter gold medal performance? Would Kamworor qualify for Kenya's Olympic team and be a podium finisher in 10,000 meters?

But on Tuesday, March 24, 2020, Japan's prime minister Shinzo Abe along with Thomas Bach, president of the International Olympic Committee, decided to postpone the Summer Olympics by a year. Concern grew as to whether the Games would even happen. Only three Olympiads in history (1916, 1940, and 1944) had ever been canceled, and all were due to war. This particular situation was unprecedented.

Though the world was forced to pause, elite athletes had to somehow continue to work through the uncertainty.

—⁂—

Four days post-surgery in June 2020, Kamworor was released from the hospital. He was restricted at home in Eldoret as his wife tended to their newborn triplets. Crutches under Kamworor's armpits would become like extensions of his body for the next two months, allowing him to at least hobble around as he hibernated inside his house. Despite the fact that he couldn't walk, he gave himself one choice: *Let me accept the situation.*

Kamworor couldn't allow himself to think for a moment that he wouldn't recover his true form. Encouraging calls from Sang as well as from the surgeon helped keep his thoughts aligned. "All will be well. You will come back stronger," training partners assured him.

After a month and a half, Kamworor could gingerly test his body by lying on the floor and doing abdominal exercises. The three-time half marathon world champ, once the world record holder in the distance, on the floor, starting over.

This is the same man whose long, muscular legs powered him through the finish line first at the New York City Marathon twice, 2017 and 2019, a rare feat at the world's largest and one of the most competitive marathons.

This is the same man who finished 11th in the 10,000 meters at the Rio Olympics in 2016. That same man has his mind set on qualifying for the Tokyo Olympics. That same man is seeking to prove he's capable of a podium finish. He has not yet captured an Olympic medal. "I must," he says.

Kamworor's team, which included Sang, a physiotherapist, his manager at Global Sports Communication, and cycling specialists, oversaw his arduous efforts to recover. Part of the rehab team had wanted Kamworor to cycle outside. "You have to explain to them, give them the picture. Some of them don't know how the set up here is," Sang said.

A typical bike in Kenya, referred to as a "Black Mamba," is heavy, basic, and gearless, primarily used to transport milk or food. The infrastructure for cycling is still very much a work in progress, incomparable to modern European cities and in the US. In Kenya, bike lanes are absent. Roads that aren't tarmac are a rocky blanket of dirt far better suited for a mountain bike than a road bike. And when you reside at least 7,800 feet above sea level in the Rift Valley, steep rolling hills are unavoidable.

Prior to 2007 Kenya had little to no cycling culture. But that year Singaporean entrepreneur Nicholas Leong founded Kenyan Riders. He wanted to build the country's first professional cycling team—and hopefully develop them to compete on the world stage. (The Tour de France is in the pipeline, a lofty goal that will require heavy investment, financially, as well as improved infrastructure.) Formerly based in Iten, then relocated to Kaptagat, the team started as a group of 16 individuals recruited to become cyclists—among them a former bicycle taxi operator and a car mechanic. Initially, they trained on cheap mountain bikes that were purchased locally.

Hopping on a road bike is not exactly a casual endeavor. For one, road bikes are still few and far between—not something one can buy easily in Kenya, both from a financial and availability standpoint. For the most part, road bikes are limited to that small percentage of professionals who specially import equipment from overseas.

Then there's the whole safety element. Any local will admit that car and motorbike drivers can be buck wild and oblivious, as Kamworor's situation attested. Also, "cows rule," they say. It's not unusual for a herd to clog the road, slowly dragging their hooves and forcing drivers to pause. Sheep and goats, too. It's the kind of experience that even a professional cyclist here in Kenya has to carefully consider. Look behind, look forward, look all around, advises John Kariuki, a member of the Kenyan Riders.

After Kamworor's rehab team better understood the situation, they resorted to importing a stationary bike that was set up inside Kamworor's home. He was instructed to cycle in low gears at first. Marc Roig, a physiotherapist who is part of the support staff for the NN Running Team and lives in Eldoret, would advise Kamworor on technique. For Kamworor, the motion of slowly circling his legs was foreign and straining, his first time ever riding a bike.

Focus on the cadence, Kamworor kept thinking.

Kamworor's muscles adopted a new rhythm after a few days, and he gradually got used to sitting in a small empty room, mundanely pedaling while listening to gospel music. "Imagine sitting," he says, "just cycling for 2 hours, 30 minutes." Going nowhere.

Sang had routinely asked Kamworor about his progress, chatting on the phone and, when the situation allowed, visiting his home. The two live three kilometers apart in Eldoret. One look from Sang, and "he can read you from head to toe," Kamworor says. If you are feeling depressed, if you are feeling challenged, "Coach," as his athletes simply refer to him, is uncannily intuitive.

From what he could see, Kamworor was not succumbing negatively to the impact of the accident. The guy was happy, Sang remembers thinking when he visited Kamworor's home. "I looked around and was talking to the wife. I was trying to test whether Geoffrey was comfortable at home under the circumstances." The circumstances included being in the company of three newborn triplets and his two other children. "You could see the wife was strong. She's a high school teacher. That helps a lot. Imagine if Geoffrey had a different wife. This woman is presenting herself as somebody in charge. She's able to handle everything. It has a positive impact."

Mental endurance, Sang says, is both innate and conditioned. "Extreme fear can have an impact on your outlook later in how you deal with things." Though Kamworor wasn't able to run, at least he could walk. Even though it was a struggle, at least he could move. Progress is progress.

But this was a slow, humbling experience for a professional athlete who was at the top of his game, requiring intense dedication to get back to the upper echelon of the sport. That is Kamworor though, driven in a hardwired way.

Kenya had named its Olympic marathon team back in January 2020. The track team, however, would be determined in June 2021, when the country would hold its Olympic Trials. The level of competition is always extreme, so much so that Kenya's Trials for athletics are described as more competitive than the actual Games.

"We cross our fingers that he'll make the Olympics," Sang says.

ROOTS

I don't like seeing people in hospitals. I don't like. I don't even . . ."
Sang pauses and clears his throat. He is a man who admittedly says,
"I try to stay away from things that are emotional. I can be too emo-
tional. I stay away from things that can take you there."

He continues, "I read a little about euthanasia, and I was trying to
understand. Initially when I was young, I thought people were stupid
to even consider it. But when you see people suffering, then you understand why some people opt for that."

Sang's mother passed away in late fall 2020. He was by her side. She
had struggled with her health after being diagnosed with diabetes in
1986. "I'd seen her suffer for a long time. I felt bad, but at the same
time, you somehow feel it's a relief for her. I've never seen somebody
who took so much pain like this lady."

After the Barcelona Olympics, Sang says he had been offered a job
as assistant coach at the University of Texas at Austin. He turned down
the opportunity. "My mom," he starts. "She was sick for a long time.
I just wanted to be close."

"When you grow up, there are certain things that you learn about life.
You place importance to certain people. I saw my mom struggle when
we were young. Then when she's sick, and you're able to support . . . you
just take off to follow money? I found it not right for me."

As for the man who was his father, whatever Sang learned from him is limited to childhood, before he turned 10 years old. Facts he knows: his father was a primary school teacher; he passed away in 1969; the death certificate gives the cause of death as cirrhosis of the liver. "That's normally associated with alcohol," Sang says.

"I think probably he had a rough life. I don't know. I never wanted to ask anybody. All I know is he was a good man, and a very respected person."

Sang's parents met in Baringo, where his mother is from. "Probably my mom was married as a second wife," he says.

Polygamy had long been a cultural practice among traditional communities in Kenya before President Uhuru Kenyatta legalized it in 2014, not without controversy. "When I was young, [in] almost every household every man had two wives." Normal, Sang adds.

"I suspected this guy must have had some problems with his first wife. That drove him into drinking. But he was a very good teacher. Then when they wanted to fire him, they transferred him to Baringo to teach. I think it was in the late '50s. And I think that's where he met my mother. But the damage was already done with the whole partaking of alcohol," Sang says.

"Alcoholism, drug abuse, those are indicators of losing hope and people who are not so sure of themselves," he continues. "Life is up and down. Some people, when they are in a downside, they give up. When you really know yourself, and you know what life is all about, it's easier to navigate those downsides."

Sang's coaching virtues are naturally a sum of life experiences—outside of running just as much as within it. Sang credits two women for shaping his etiquette, ethical standards, and character. "My mother, my grandmother from my mother's side, brought me serious values," Sang says. When he reflects on the matriarch of his upbringing, his voice holds a particular space as he speaks of his mother's mother.

She had a natural language of sage counsel and an intuitive mind—the kind that could sense even from afar when the young Patrick was about to show up at her door. She would "feel it in her blood," as Sang puts it of the influential woman whom he says had lived beyond 100 years old.

"I learned a lot from her," Sang says about his grandmother. "She would always tell me so many things about how to deal with human beings. I'm so grateful."

Sang continues to focus inward. "I look at myself. Am I satisfied with who I am? If I'm satisfied, then I'm sure wherever I started the journey genetically, they were okay," he says. *Okay* as in a good person of the world. "I always try to be happy. But happiness is not about what I have. It's about how I feel when I'm in this world."

Just one in-depth conversation with Sang can unveil his honest ways of living. Words slip out like strokes of a painting and hint of the learned sensibility that poured into his life growing up. The words *honest* and *trust* surface often in his conversations, like permanent vocabulary.

Every athlete at camp regurgitates them too: "Always be honest—to yourself, to other people, to your family, to your body," says Kamworor, words he learned from Sang.

There's another layer to Sang's guidance about how to exist.

"This is a difficult world," he says. "The challenge is to have more light than darkness."

"Tenda wema nenda zako." Sang speaks the phrase in Swahili.

Do what is right and go your way.

The Highlands are good for the lungs. But also hard on the lungs. There's a dirt hill leading into Kaptagat Forest. Sang points. "That hill, it will pump enough oxygen out of your brain." He laughs. It's true.

The high altitude can easily steal your breath. But the expressionless faces of runners out here hint little, if at all, that the thin air is boxing with their lungs. Training at high altitude is hard enough if one is in shape—and unimaginably demanding when one isn't.

So just think about having to rebuild your endurance while living at high altitude after being inactive for three months, then after several weeks of rehab. For Kamworor, there is no alternative.

He has been gifted with time due to the effects of the pandemic pushing the Summer Games a year. Had the Olympics been held when originally scheduled starting in July 2020, it would have been outside of the realm of possibility for him. But now, there's still a chance to go to Tokyo—so long as he can get back to form. Then, so long as he can qualify for Kenya's Olympic team at the country's highly competitive trials in June 2021. Then, so long as he can remain healthy in the weeks leading into the Olympics. And only then can he place his feet on the starting line in the 10,000 final, the first track and field medal event of the Games. The 25-lap race will be held on July 30, 2021.

The process of getting there is a delicate art of staying present and focused. Two months ago, Kamworor was able to get back on his feet. He could start running. Or rather, relearn how to run. His body refused to move at any other pace but slowly, sustaining him just enough for 10 minutes, then a minute walking, a pattern that he gradually increased.

His muscles continued to pump, and by December 2020 Kamworor was finally able to run. Kind of. He starts "small" by his standards, 10 kilometers at a time. Six miles and change is hardly the distance he is used to logging, sometimes upward of 40 kilometers (roughly 25 miles) with wide, effortless strides—the very definition of poetry in motion.

Sang had purposely wanted Kamworor to talk about his experience "as an encouragement to others that even when you think you are down, you're not down," he says. That's the picture he wanted to paint, a two-pronged intention. One, to give people hope. Two, to realize that injuries are normal. "Part of the best way to heal is to share," Sang comments.

Running doesn't exactly feel effortless at the moment. It feels arduous. Kamworor can feel a painful sensation arresting his leg. He feels like the muscles have shortened. Doctors tell him it's normal. He hasn't run in so long. Too long. The leg is trying to adjust. He is trying to adjust.

This is the same guy who was in New York City 13 months ago reclaiming his title at the largest major marathon in the world. The same Geoffrey who darted in Central Park to break the tape at the finish line like someone running toward the end zone to score a touchdown. The way his lithe legs moved fluidly with a powerful and smooth cadence. The way his lungs carried air from the immense stamina claimed at 2,400 meters. The way his mind carried hope.

Kamworor's mind still carries hope as he alternates running 10 kilometers one day, then resting the following day. Sore. And in a lot of pain. Though not discouraged. *Never.* His words again. Marginal gains.

Kenya's Olympic Trials are six months out. There's room for progress. But to what level can he bring his endurance, speed, and strength?

January 2021. The beginning of the new year is always a time to uplift, take charge, set goals, revise one's perspective. How do you want to better yourself? And what can you do each day to get to where you want to be? Kamworor's mind has clear direction: have patience, be persistent, stay hopeful. "Grab a higher branch" is an analogy both he and Kipchoge use. Move forward.

And he does. This new year promises to be different than the last. Different is open to interpretation. Kamworor's training continues to progress. Initially, the act of moving his body seems to worsen the pain in his leg. Still, he runs. Farther—20 kilometers, then 25 kilometers.

One day, Kamworor goes out for what's supposed to be 10 kilometers. *The leg doesn't feel so bad*, he thinks. So he continues. Another kilometer. One more. One more! Two more! Five more! Sweat cascades down his face as he brings his body to 20 kilometers, the equivalent of 12.4 miles. He is earning back his endurance. The leg feels okay. No pain.

So he keeps going. "Today, I must do 30 kilometers," he thinks. *Must*. Kamworor continues. Another kilometer. Another. One becomes two becomes five becomes five more. He brings his body to 30 kilometers. The leg still feels okay.

What. Did. He. Just. Do?

Kamworor versus Kamworor. And Kamworor comes out on top as a better version of himself. Happiness.

He shares the news with everyone at camp, with Sang and with his doctor. Shared happiness.

"It seems it's a new beginning." Kamworor says the words out loud.

The following day, he steps out of bed. Throbbing pain, a searing beating rhythm in his leg. The muscles are still adjusting. *Accept this situation.*

Five months out until Kenya's Olympic Trials.

—⁓—

Thomas Bach, president of the International Olympic Committee, had stated on January 21, 2021, there would be no plan B. The Summer Olympics would be held, but under highly regulated protocol, which would include frequent testing onsite for COVID-19 in addition to before and after arrival in Japan.

The following month, the blue gate leading into the training camp ushers in its residents. The feeling of coming back to home away from home is precious, like reuniting with people who are a collected family. Camp member Victor Chumo describes it as a sigh of relief. Joy. A slice of normalcy in what is still a chaotic and uncertain situation all over the world. The pandemic took a mental toll on many people, these athletes included. The value of teamwork was exceptionally clear when they arrived at camp after 10 months away.

"Being back is good," Kipchoge says. "It's good to come back and pick up training again and have a normal life. This is our normal life, what we are doing."

Back to the dormitory-style rooms, each shared with a teammate. Back to the dining area for meals of ugali and sukuma wiki and stacks of warm, flaky chapati, cups of creamy and sweet chai made with fresh milk, shared over conversations in person and not through WhatsApp texts or video calls. Back to training, thin silhouettes of future world and Olympic champions running next to some current world and Olympic champions.

To be back, though, means to be careful and to follow new rules dictated by the pandemic. While Sang allows his athletes to train together, "we are in a bubble. There's minimal outside interaction." The athletes cannot afford to be risky as some prepare for the Olympics.

Kamworor continues to follow a training program. He can hit the targets. Though he feels a little pain in his leg, at least he can progress through the program. The pain subsides by mid-February, four months out from Kenya's Olympic Trials and five and a half months out from the start of the men's 10,000 meters in Tokyo.

FULL CIRCLE

Qatar Airways flight QR1341 lands at Jomo Kenyatta International Airport in Nairobi just shy of midnight on March 2, 2021. Vital cargo. One million COVID-19 vaccines, made available through COVAX as part of a global initiative for equitable access.

Three days later, on a Friday, Sang runs for an hour in Eldoret. "Just jogging," he says. "For my age, you need to go slow," he says, laughing. He doesn't miss being a competitive athlete. *Not really.* His words. It's been a long time since his last competition on the track, the one on August 12, 1998, a Diamond League meet in Zurich. Sang flew in his college coach James Blackwood all the way from Texas.

When Blackwood arrived in Switzerland, Sang hadn't mentioned to him that this meet was to be his last. He was going to retire. He had simply told Blackwood, "Coach, I want you to be in Zurich on this day for a few days. I'm paying for everything."

"He spent a fortune," Blackwood remembers. A business class plane ticket. A fancy hotel room. Shuffled around in a Mercedes. "The whole nine yards," he chuckles. "That was a great, great trip. We were close, there's no doubt about it."

Sang continues. "The guy was very happy. I ran 8:08, one of the fastest times. I was number two in the race." Blackwood went crazy,

Sang says, still smiling at the fact. He ran like a madman from the stands all the way to the infield. Security chased him. "No! That's my boy! That's my boy!" Blackwood screamed the kind of proud scream that a father would for a son.

"I was telling him, this is the journey you started." Sang's eyes begin to well. "It was the only thing I could do for him."

The cycle was complete. Here were two men who each took a chance on the other. Had faith in each other. And trusted the journey.

That journey for Sang started as a standout collegiate athlete who went on to become a gold medalist at the 1987 All-Africa Games. He had podium finishes at two World Championships with a silver medal dangling from his neck on both occasions (1991 in Tokyo and 1993 in Stuttgart, Germany). He then made two appearances at the Summer Olympics—including helping Kenya sweep the podium in the steeplechase for the first time in history in 1992.

That journey brought Sang all over the world to race not just in the steeplechase, but in various distances, from a 10-mile road race in Nebraska, to 5,000 meters in Sweden and Switzerland (post-retirement, Sang transitioned to running half marathons and eventually marathons around Europe).

That journey repeatedly tested Sang's fortitude. And he repeatedly proved he could always measure up.

Here is where the chapter ends, the one where that feeling of being on the starting line, eyes intensely staring ahead, ears tuning in and tuning out the noise of the crowd, will no longer be as a professional athlete. The nature of the sport is that the lifeline ends. And one must pivot. Sang's about-face would bring him back to the starting line though as a coach. And he would keep Blackwood's advice close. "I told him listen to your athlete, and he will listen to you," Blackwood recalls relaying to Sang. "You've got to listen to him. You can't tell him, 'this is the way that we're going to do it.' It's critically important."

Asked what he noticed about Sang that gave him the impression he could become a good coach, "Toughness. He was so tough. So mentally tough," Blackwood says.

Though he is 80 years old, Blackwood doesn't have to shake his memory about "let me tell you" stories, watching Sang in college develop as an athlete and as a man. Once, in 1986 at the Penn Relays, the oldest and largest track and field competition in the US, Sang won the steeplechase (the 8:31.1 he clocked still ranks third of all-time in Penn Relays history). A race tradition is that a winning athlete is awarded a gold watch.

Many moons prior, Blackwood had run in the Penn Relays on the distance medley relay when he was a collegiate athlete at Abilene Christian University. He had finished second. No watch.*

Sang turned to Blackwood in the stands. "Coach! You never won one of these. Take this," he said, tossing Blackwood a small box.

"He was very easy to coach. No doubt," Blackwood says. "He listened. I listened to him. The important thing for me as a coach is listening to the athlete, knowing what they are thinking, what they are doing. What is important to them, what's good for them."

Compared to his athletes, running for Sang serves a different purpose now. "I believe in God," Sang has said more than once. "I think my best moments are communicated with God when I'm running."

Running is also one of the things he does to quell stress. His calm demeanor doesn't suggest that he experiences much of it. But yes, even Sang at times can feel it—not personally, he clarifies, "but as a responsibility, as a person who is supposed to be responsible."

"I think stress is healthy sometimes. It gives you a push," he says.

Outside of running, he points to reading and naps as ways that help manage any stress he does feel. "I actually don't like stress myself. I'm

---

* The runner-up receives a silver medal; third place, a bronze medal. The latter two are traditional offerings.

a realist. If there's no answer to anything that's complicated, just leave it. Why should I struggle?" Sang says.

He uses the word *therapeutic* when he talks about running. "Whenever I run, I always pray. I always confess. I correct myself. Whatever I'd done wrong. I get the right answers. I find myself apologizing," he says. Sang doesn't let on any specifics, just that running affords a space for him to "get all sorts of solutions."

The distance he runs doesn't matter. "I actually don't measure. I normally go out between 40 minutes and 1 hour 10," Sang says. "Just to feel good." He runs alone and at least three times a week, never at a specific time, but rather when time allows. "Sometimes I run at odd hours," he says. "I don't have a regularized program. I used to run early in the morning, but now my body doesn't want to go with that routine."

After this particular hour run, he speaks of the COVID situation in Kenya. "We have yo-yo type of infection rates," he states. "Sometimes it's down; now I see it going up again."

On March 5, 2021, three days after the vaccines arrived in Kenya, they began to be administered. Currently, organizers of the Tokyo Olympics are not mandating shots for those participating in the Games.

"I wish it was compulsory," Sang says.

"Going toward the Olympics, first of all we are not so sure whether the Olympics will be on. We program ourselves that it will be. That makes it easier to plan and to train. You have a target. So you plan to be at the peak. At the moment, unless they start talking about 'may not,' that's when the confusion starts. But at the moment, we are focusing," he says.

STAKES

He loves to run. It feels natural, the way his feet greet the ground with each step, as though making friends with the earth. His stride is long and perfectly cadenced. Graceful, like a form of art. He likes being outside, moving alongside the arcadian rhythm of life with fresh air filling his lungs, creating an internal orchestra pulsing in his chest. When he runs it's like something releases, an intangible and addictive sensation. Running doesn't define him, but life feels thrown off-kilter without this pure stimulus that leads to a sense of freedom. Without this pure stimulus that experiments with his willpower.

When you are young, you run simply for joy, detached from stakes and pressure. You run blissfully unaware of what the sport actually is, but as they say in Swahili, "pole pole," that is *slowly*, you figure things out. What distance suits you? Where is your boundary? Can you push it? If and when you do, what will be the consequence of that? The consequence of your talent? The consequence of your ambition?

"God," Sang says, "will never give you talent for free. There's a purpose. The way you use it will determine what happens to you."

What gradation is your will? What gradation is your commitment? What gradation is your focus?

As you mature from youth to adult, for a finite percentage of young runners with promise, you still run to figure things out, like how far can that boundary stretch? Can you keep pushing that boundary to get to the upper echelon of the sport? Can you become the sport's next king (or queen)? Can you become the next Kipchoge?

The consequences of your talent can lead to a high stake. Correction: *stakes*. Plural. Will you be a dominant star? Do you have the personal commitment, mental fortitude, and physical aptitude to do it? You have to figure out how well and for how long you can engage in the high-level physiological and psychological dance.

Life as a runner in the exclusive elite club is its own race—against time. That is, the narrow window of your life when you have an opportunity to "make it," to put a number on the clock reflective of your stature, to stake your place in the running pantheon. And to become somebody that people remember. And if you become somebody that people remember, will you also become somebody that people respect—not just as an athlete, but as a person?

Kamworor is in the midst of writing this influential chapter of his life.

Mid-March, Kamworor got a flu, "very strong" he said for scale. "It's a panicky situation," Sang says. "It was a very bad cold." Kamworor almost had to withdraw from competition. He was sickened enough to warrant a visit to the hospital, where he was told he had an infection. *An infection*, three days prior to traveling to Turkey to run the Istanbul Half Marathon, his first international race since November 2019, when he won the New York City Marathon.

And that was a stronger version of Kamworor. Pre-accident. Pre-surgery, pre-stitches, pre-crutches. That version of Kamworor knew how to win. This version of Kamworor is resetting and therefore having to prove something about himself to himself. And effectively, whether or not he wants to, he is also proving something to the world—that one can crash but not burn. Instead, one can get up and carry on winning. Kamworor is hopeful, at least.

Before he leaves for Turkey, he is urging his body to get healthy. This body has already been urging itself to recover. For months. Life with crutches. Life on a stationary bike pedaling in two-and-a-half-hour increments, going nowhere, yet somewhere. One gingerly step, followed by a cautious run, and eventually teasing his legs just as much as his mind with a kilometer more, a kilometer more. A kilometer more.

An embodiment of resilience, otherwise defined as "the capability of a strained body to recover its size and shape after deformation caused especially by compressive stress." Is this the definition of the new Geoffrey Kamworor?

The Istanbul Half Marathon is part of his equation to return to pre-accident Kamworor. The one who has experienced the delicate feeling of the finish line tape brushing against his chest. The one who is respected for his fine marriage of endurance and speed, so synced that he delivered a half marathon world record, 58:01, in September 2019 in Copenhagen, the same place where he won his first world title five years prior.

He's been groomed to compete. *"I must go. I must do it."* A self-induced order. He takes a cocktail of antibiotics and painkillers, attempting to dull the flu symptoms and revive his achy muscles. Physically, he is tired. But mentally, he tells himself he is strong.

So he gets on the plane, bypassing the aches. Or rather, semi-ignoring them for now. When he arrives in Turkey a few days in advance of the Istanbul Half Marathon, he still feels tired, his muscles feel weak. But he is already here. So he *must do it.*

Kamworor has primed himself for this moment to test where his boundary is, and whether he can push it, after more than a year away from international competition and after months of recovering from a devastating accident.

Never mind that his muscles still feel sore when he wakes up on race day. "I must do a good result." Words he thought pre-race as his name is hyped. Eyes are on him.

In Istanbul, eyes are also on Kenyan Kibiwott Kandie, the guy who replaced Kamworor's half marathon world record just a few months prior, in December 2020. The current record holder will clash with the previous, as the media put it. Both Kandie and Kamworor head-line the race. The shape is really good, Kamworor had said about his build-up to this half marathon. He felt okay until that flu.

Why is he even here?

The consequences of his position. The stakes. He needs to get this racing experience under his feet, he'll say. The Olympic mentality is too ingrained. "I knew this might be the last road race before I compete in the Olympics. I just have to show up."

Before he competes in the Olympics.

He's not on Kenya's Olympic team yet, but his mind seems to have already decided.

So he plants his feet on the starting line, April 4, 2021, a Sunday. And he runs. Or rather, races. More appropriate, considering what he clocks, 59:38. Runner-up, just three seconds behind the winner.

"I'm coming back!" Words he not only silently thinks, but also says out loud.

This is what happens when you show up for yourself. Day after day. Week after week. Month after month. When you keep your head up.

Months ago, he couldn't walk. Months ago, his exceptional speed, endurance, and fitness were forced to hibernate as he rehabbed and diligently concentrated on nurturing it all back.

"It's good to see him come back," Sang says.

And now, somehow, Kamworor is going to get to the starting line of the Olympic Trials and ultimately to the starting line of the 10,000 meters final at the Olympic Games.

That's the plan.

"What is there is beyond your control," Sang says, a lesson he learned during his youth. "Do your best. There's nothing else."

At least what Kamworor can control is staying committed to his dream. Every day he wakes up, this is what he chooses. Every day.

COURTESY OF

"That vehicle you see there," Sang points, "Eliud bought it. That was in 2019."

It is slick and shiny, and even two years later still carries the scent of newness. At the time, it was the latest Mercedes on the market. The luxury vehicle was delivered on a truck to Sang's house in Eldoret. Zero mileage.

"I think he sensed something," Kipchoge says of his surprise gift to his lifelong coach.

Sang remembers asking him why.

"He was saying he is who he is because of me. So it's nothing," Sang says. After he received the unexpected and extravagant offering, Sang asked everyone in his family to call Kipchoge.

Kipchoge smiles widely from the flashback of picking up his cell phone and hearing their voices. "Patrick has surpassed 50 years," Kipchoge says. "He deserves to relax and enjoy the Mercedes." Kipchoge keeps going. "He has a problem with the neck and the back." A Mercedes is good for that, he adds.

The rationale is deeper than that, though. "My idea really was to say thank you," Kipchoge says of the gift he offered after Sang coached him through breaking the two-hour barrier for the marathon. "I think he deserves more."

"My life is different because," Kipchoge pauses. "I don't know how father love looks like." He pauses again.

"I was taken care of by one parent, which is okay. Patrick has guided me life-wise, sport-wise, business-wise. Dos and don'ts," Kipchoge says. "He guided me the way he guides his kids."

Kipchoge uses the label "life coach" when he speaks of Sang, whom he simply refers to as Patrick. "He acted like my father. He showed me the way, what to do, what not to do as far as to have the right values in your mind."

The word *honest* is mentioned. Live an honest life. Kipchoge repeats out loud Sang's advice. "An honest life is you have one face, not two. When I am at home, I'm Eliud. When I'm in Nairobi, I am the same person. When I am in London, I am the same person. When I am in the Caribbean, I am the same person. It means you need to have that face everywhere. Live an honest life." No matter where you are in the world, no matter who you are with in the world.

"I would like other people in my life to be that—themselves, their true self and nothing else. You cannot be what society wants you to be. If you try to do it, you'll be lost," Sang says.

Sang found that honesty in his own years as an athlete was the only way he was able to thrive, and he has expanded upon that in his coaching. The beginning of successful coaching, as far as coach-athlete relationships, is when the coach has the trust of an athlete. "The trust that you get from anybody is something that's processed through a mental engagement within an individual," he says.

"Once you have the trust, then you're on board together. If that person gives you total trust, if you push that person, they will never ask why you are pushing them. So what is the limiting factor in that process? It's a lack of mental engagement. But if you have given me the trust, you'll have gone through the process," Sang says. "This guy understands where I came from. And he's done something to me to get the concept of the impact of my background. And this process gives you a window to see. And by seeing, you internalize."

Sang knows Kipchoge's values are directly related to their bond. Coaching, Sang says, can come across like parenting, but it's not the same. "In the professional world of athletics or any sport, the only values that you bring that are related to parenting is that you're hanging together," he says.

Just as a parent must show care to a child, a coach must show care to an athlete. Coaching, like parenting, requires patience and understanding. "Those values are cross cutting," Sang says. "But at the end of the day, the difference is that the person in the sport has to know where they are going."

"As a parent, you deal with your children within the context of being a parent. When children are children, they don't know where they are going. So it's like you with a torch showing them. In professional sports, the child, who is the athlete now, should know where they are going. *Should.* And if they know where they are going, they should know the nature of the thing they are engaging in," Sang says.

"In the case of parenting, you're literally taking somebody by the hand and saying, 'this is where we are going.'" He continues, "I always tell athletes, tell me the destination, and I'll help you get there."

Sang's runners use the word *father* as one description of him, though. "I respect him so much because he has always been there for us. He always makes sure that he's on time. He has never missed any program. Actually, he's like our father," Kamworor says. "He always makes sure that we are taken care of. He makes sure that we are comfortable, we train very well. We never lack anything."

After Sang received the car from Kipchoge, he drove around with his son. "Within a few hours I was getting phone calls," Sang says. "These people only worship people with class and what is considered the objects of vanity." It was a lesson, he says, for his son.

"Eliud does not have a car like that," Sang says. "He drives a pickup."

A MARATHON MISSION

The NN Mission Marathon, a one-off competition just for elites, was scheduled to take place in Hamburg, Germany, on a closed circuit in the city center, April 11, 2021.

But the world changes. And it changes fast.

Germany's chancellor Angela Merkel had announced that the country's lockdown measures would be extended due to an unrelenting resurgence of the coronavirus. Local COVID-19 restrictions tightened, and the government pulled the plug two weeks before the race, leaving organizers scrambling to move the marathon to another venue on April 18, a week later than originally planned.

Reorganizing the marathon at Twente Airport in Enschede, the Netherlands, in 12 days required a herculean effort by three organizations—Global Sports Communication, the NN Running Team, and the Hamburg Marathon—in order to offer 70 invite-only athletes, mostly from Europe and East Africa, the rare chance to race. Given that elites have had few opportunities to compete since the start of the pandemic, the event is a crucial last chance for some of the participants to attempt an Olympic-qualifying performance (though that doesn't automatically grant them a spot on their respective federation's team).

Eyes worldwide are on Kipchoge, as they always are, but particularly now. Six months prior in London, he had stunned the running world by not winning for the first time in seven years. Kipchoge had dropped from the lead pack during mile 24 (of 26.2) and wasn't able to regain contact, finishing eighth overall and more than a minute behind winner Shura Kitata of Ethiopia.

Get up and forget, though.

"The past is past. What you have in control is what comes." Kipchoge believes in the present moment. And what's in his control at this moment is this race today, April 18, 2021, four months out from defending his Olympic marathon title in Japan.

"It's good to happen. It's good actually to run as one. It's good to show the world that even in the mid of the pandemic, in the mid of hard times in this world, we can still run," he said during a virtual press conference two days before the event. "We're in a new transition towards the future." *He* is in a transition, too.

Curious minds the world over want to know, *how well can Kipchoge still run?*

He arrived a few days before the race, his first time in Enschede, but not within vicinity in Hengelo, where he ran his personal best in 10,000 meters in 2007 (26:49.02), and his personal best in 1,500 meters in 2004 (3:33.20).

Kipchoge is joined by partners from training camp, including Jonathan Korir, Laban Korir, and Augustine Choge—all of whom will race. They are accompanied by Sang.

"It's different. Different mindset," Sang says about when he travels to a race in support of his athletes. "You're more or less thinking about other people, whereas when you are competing, you're thinking about yourself."

The dynamics as a coach put him on constant alert. *"Am I going to wake up tomorrow to an athlete complaining?"* is one thought among many.

Getting here was an undertaking itself, requiring a specific procedure taken via a nasal swab referred to as a polymerase chain reaction (PCR) test for COVID-19. A negative result is obligatory to exit and enter Kenya and also to participate in the NN Mission Marathon. That preceded a one-hour domestic flight from Eldoret to Nairobi, then an eight-and-a-half-hour flight to Amsterdam, followed by a two-hour drive to Enschede. All in an effort to run 42.1 kilometers (26.2 miles). In circles.

The course is held on an airfield, advantageous for the athletes. A flat route is sure to be a fast route. Each competitor will trace the 5K loop approximately eight times.

Kipchoge is targeting 2:05:30. That equates to running a mile in roughly 4 minutes and 47 seconds. Not many people are capable of clocking just one mile at such a pace. Kipchoge must do it 26 times consecutively, plus that 0.2 extra (321.8 meters, if you're into specifics).

Kipchoge and the lead group, which includes Jonathan Korir and three pacers, take off and stream through the first 5K in 14 minutes and 54 seconds, on target to meet the goal. Of course, this is early—too early to judge an end result.

Training partners turned competitors Kipchoge and Korir continue running side by side, the only two to brave the 2:05 effort as they establish a sizable gap between the rest of the field. The weather is gray, dreary—typical Dutch conditions, though there is no rain at the moment. The two men are dressed identically: skin-tight black shorts, white racerback tank, white arm sleeves.

They pass through another 5K split, 14:21. Kipchoge, looking relaxed in true form, is still on track for his target time. In fact, he's beginning to get ahead of it.

By 15K, he and Korir hit 43:46, just outside of 2:03 pace. One pacemaker drops out halfway through the race. Kipchoge and Korir keep the tempo. Not many are able to ever run such a time, even just for a short while. But Kipchoge and Korir maintain the pace, confidently and comfortably. It is what makes them "the real wheat."

The world can collectively sigh with relief that the sport's king is performing at the standard we are used to seeing him run. How comforting for those who thought him less capable since his London performance months back in October 2020. But anything can still happen. That's the thing about the marathon. It can be predictably unpredictable. It's often said that the last few miles of a marathon are the most telling, when the race truly begins. It is a state of the race when life pokes one's mental endurance just as much as one's physical endurance. How the mind retaliates can have an impressionable effect on the body.

Kipchoge knows this mind-body balance at play. "The moment you lose even 0.01 [percent], then you are done," he says. The moment you want to recover is a moment you lose a lot of energy. "You'll remove the energy from your muscles to your mind. Then you'll be tired in thinking and physically tired. It's good to actually be on the course. Just be there," Kipchoge says. Being there allows him to preserve his mental energy—a major factor of the marathon. And mental energy is necessary for physical energy. "When you lose one, the other goes out."

Kipchoge runs on the heels of a pacer, with Korir on the side. "Still here!" a commentator says, toned as though a little in disbelief about Korir, who carries his arms high as he keeps up. Meanwhile, Kipchoge appears to be rationing his speed endurance. Push hard, but not too hard and not too early. Managing the mind-body dynamics during a marathon is an art.

Kipchoge's and Korir's arms mirror each other, swinging across their chests in even cadence. The way their feet stamp the ground perfectly in step, it's as though their strides have been cloned. They are in sync until something gives. Or rather, someone gives.

Stride for stride for stride. Kipchoge is pulling ahead of his training partner and friend. In a matter of seconds, Kipchoge and Korir are no longer running side by side. Mental and physical rationing pays off.

Kipchoge is steady as he continues faster than Korir—and faster than every other entrant in the field. And it's the pacemaker who trails behind Kipchoge rather than leading him.

Forget about last fall. *Defeated. Beaten. Dethroned.* Piranha descriptors that appeared in media headlines after Kipchoge's loss in London. "I trained 100 percent. But something came in. That's how life is," Kipchoge said of that race. Here, at Twente Airport, formerly a military airfield and now "where planes come to end their lives," as a commentator put it, Kipchoge is rewriting the narrative.

Kipchoge runs as though he's cruising. Yes, this is still effort, as much as he makes this appear effortless. His white tank clings to his body, gently flapping at his hips. His heels kick up from behind, a sign that his body is still very much present, moving with purpose.

He flows through toward the finish ahead of the motorbike. Sang stands at the line holding one side of the winners tape, his face covered with a white KN95 mask as Kipchoge runs through it, raising his arms victoriously above his head. The clock reads 2:04:30, two minutes ahead of runner-up Korir, who achieved a personal best.

A page has turned.

Kipchoge doesn't believe in failure. He believes in moving forward. "If you fail, it's not that you are on a cliff and you are gone. It's just a challenge as far as life is concerned," Kipchoge says. "You wake up again and move on."

He continues. "Even with UFC in the US, somebody's going to training camp for months, and tomorrow he will be knocked out in 18 seconds. But he's still waking up, going to training camp again and fighting."

Failing is not really failing; it's navigating a challenge. "Just wake up and try to navigate, but don't just accept to fail," Kipchoge says.

Later, he tells of an incident that occurred roughly 15 miles into the race. "You know what happened?" Kipchoge asks. His stomach was not good, as he put it. "It was really terrible. There was no way . . . it just came out, and I had to run," Kipchoge says.

He had been preparing for the race for four months. He wasn't about to downgrade his effort. "Then it will take me another five months to have another race," he says. "All my clothes were really dirty, but I moved on. I had to rush to press conference, rush to the hotel to take a shower. Everything was a mess. But I blocked. I don't care."

Just move on. The power of the mind, he says.

haba na haba hujaza kibaba

little by little fills the pot

KEEPING THE FAITH

Heavy rains have saturated the dry grassy field at the training camp, leaving the soft rusty-red soil slightly squishy. It was barely 54 degrees Fahrenheit by the time Faith Kipyegon had slipped her braided hair into a ponytail and outfitted her 5-foot-2, 100-pound body in maroon running tights, fluorescent yellow knee-high socks, a purple jacket and a pair of Nikes. She steps onto the 380-meter dirt track, stripped of white lines with the exception of a faded one along the perimeter.

Kipyegon jogs counterclockwise with two camp mates, warming up for the workout. Tuesday mornings are one of the hardest sessions of the week, and this day in April 2021 calls for 2 × 2,000 meters, 2 × 1,200 meters, followed by 3 × 600 meters.

By 10 A.M. Kipyegon peels off her warm-up clothes and begins her first rep. She clicks the start button on her watch and takes off sprinting. Her bubblegum-pink short-sleeved shirt and matching arm warmers make her easy to spot among 30 men running around the track. The sound of long, lean legs stampeding on the ground cuts the silence in this countryside corner of Kaptagat.

"Mtarudia!" assistant coach Richard Metto says. *You will repeat.*

Metto is tall, and though lanky, he has the kind of towering frame that belongs to a basketball player. He can easily intimidate. His voice carries a businesslike tone. When he speaks, one listens. *Must.* When he gives direction, one does as instructed. *Must.* Sang met his right-hand man in Italy in the 1980s. Metto was a former athlete, competitive in 10,000 meters. He knows the game. He knows the stakes. As much as Sang is serious on the field, so too is Metto. He is the kind of authority figure one does not want to disappoint.

So when he calls out a directive, the athlete understands it's in their best interest to follow suit. In this case, the distance was somehow miscalculated. Kipyegon's group had run 400 meters shy of the expected 2,000. "Tutaanza upya," Kipyegon says. *We will start afresh.*

She takes off again, led by her pacer, a man named Bernard Soi, who has aided her for the past eight years. Kipyegon kicks her heels up with power. She strides with authority as beads of sweat on her forehead sparkle in the soft morning light. When she finishes the rep, she lifts her shirt to wipe the salty dew, slightly revealing a sign of motherhood. Two years ago, in June 2018, Kipyegon gave birth to her first child, Alyn, by cesarean delivery.

Her daughter is 25 kilometers away in Eldoret, where her husband Timothy Kitum, an Olympic bronze medalist in the 800 meters, lives and helps take care of Alyn. Kipyegon will see her family in a few days, when she leaves the training camp on her lone day off. While it's not easy being away from Alyn six days a week, for Kipyegon it is the only way to live at the moment. The 27-year-old is three months away from the start of the Tokyo Olympics, and she is aiming to become the second woman in history to win back-to-back Olympic titles for the 1,500 meters.

The second youngest of nine children, Faith Chepngetich Kipyegon grew up 150 miles south of Kaptagat in Bomet, Kenya, as the daughter of two farmers. A soccer player while in primary school, Kipyegon was introduced to running during gym class when she was 14 years old. She won a 1-kilometer race, which gave her the impression that she had potential in the sport and it was worth exploring. She ran barefoot.

Her entrance into international competitions came quickly. At 16, she traveled to Bydgoszcz, Poland, where she finished fourth in the U-20 race of the 2010 World Cross Country Championships, much to her surprise. A year later, in Punta Umbria, Spain, she won the U-20 title.

Next came Lille, France, for the 2011 World Youth Championships, her first European track race (she had raced 1,500 meters in Kenya, finishing third at the World Junior Championship Trials in Nairobi). More gold for Kipyegon, in 1,500 meters (and a course record). Kipyegon's talent in the event was further revealed when she set the national junior record for 1,500 meters in 2012 in Shanghai. A national junior title followed, along with a place on Kenya's team for the 2012 London Olympics. She was 18.

Kipyegon's bid to compete in the 1,500-meter final at the Games fell short when she finished seventh in her heat.[*] In 2015, Dutchman Bram Som, former European outdoor 800 meter champion, began coaching her virtually, instructing her workouts through text messages. She'd train with a pacemaker, then report back. Som oversaw all aspects of her program, from Kipyegon's recovery routine to her nutrition.

After Kipyegon won the 1,500 meter title at the 2016 Rio Olympics, her first Olympic gold, she had planned to start a family and factored in having adequate time to recover and aim for the 2019 World Championships in Doha, Qatar. She became pregnant after the 2017 World Championships in London. After giving birth in June 2018, Kipyegon spent the next eight months resting and enjoying motherhood without pressuring herself to return to competition.

When Kipyegon married, she had decided to move from her training base in Keringet in Nakuru County, to Eldoret, where she and her husband could be closer to Kitum's family. She opted to switch coaches, too, and joined Sang's enclave in February 2019.

---

[*] Six of the first nine finishers of of the women's 1,500 meter final at the 2012 London Olympics were later linked to performance-enhancing drugs in the years preceding and also after the competition.

Sang guided Kipyegon as she came back from maternity leave and shed the 40-pound weight gain from her pregnancy. "Imagine!" she says. One can't when you see her lean petite body in person.

"It's really not easy to recover after a C-section," Kipyegon says. The wound from the surgical procedure can feel painful and swollen, and healing can take several weeks. "He told me I have to come back slowly." *Train wisely* was the direction. Rebuilding cannot be rushed. One must consider the big picture. Too much too soon can be more damaging for an athlete, potentially leading to problems that can set them back. Moving forward is a process that requires patience.

"Sometimes he can be tough," Kipyegon says of Sang. "But he is a really nice coach."

"He knows everything. He reads your mind before you tell what you have in the mind," Kipyegon says.

Getting her fitness back starting in February 2019 involved walking before graduating to gentle 20-minute jogs until her body was strong enough to rebuild her speed. She progressed through Sang's training program, pushing herself through tiring long runs and gym sessions multiple times a week. That her daughter was well taken care of by family allowed Kipyegon to focus on her training and rest when she needed.

By fall of 2019, Kipyegon had primed herself for the World Championships in Doha. Much to her surprise, she ran a personal best of 3:54 and collected a silver medal—and set a Kenyan national record. It was a milestone that not only built her confidence, but also proved that motherhood hasn't slowed her down.

Kipyegon has been practically unbeatable throughout her career. Described by the media as "Kenya's golden girl," she is uniquely qualified for the title.

"Superstar!" Sang calls her. He whips out his phone and doesn't hesitate to feverishly scroll through it in search of an image noting that Kipyegon was recognized among the 20 most influential women in Kenya, as named by Woman Kenya Network in 2021. He smiles proudly, clearly tickled: "The most influential women in Kenya!" In March 2021, First Lady Margaret Kenyatta also recognized Kipyegon among other Kenyan women athletes for their perseverance, sacrifice, and commitment.

"When I see my daughter, she gives me motivation," Kipyegon says. Her world-class training is exhausting, but so is parenting. "I have to balance both," she says. What keeps her going is the insatiable need to offer Alyn a better life than the one Kipyegon experienced growing up. "It was not easy for my mother and father," Kipyegon offers.

While she doesn't use the label *poor*, she offers that money was always tight. Sometimes there wasn't enough to afford school fees. It was, she admits, a struggle; Kipyegon says she is the first in her family to finish school. But she is not the first to run. Her father, Samuel Koech, competed in the 400 meters and 800 meters as a youth, and her older sister, Beatrice Mutai, specializes in 10 kilometers and the half marathon.

Kipyegon wants to enroll her daughter in private school, unlike the education she herself received. When Kipyegon gets up at 5:40 A.M. each day, her motive is unspoken.

"I see where I came from, and I see where my daughter is. It's a little bit different," Kipyegon says. "That teaches me that I have to work hard to provide her more things that I didn't get."

SOW

The moon clings to morning as the day begins to awaken, spreading hues of lilac in the sky.

This is the slice of the day when a younger version of Sang would run. "Before I became anybody, when I was at home, I would make sure I would run before dawn. You don't want people to see you run, because they think that people who ran were not smart enough." An opinion across the board, he says.

But he was an A-level student, and he proved otherwise. Then he could train anytime, because he busted the myth that only less intelligent people run or participate in sports. "I could run in my village, and I'm sure that's when people like Eliud could see me."

While Kipchoge doesn't recall specifics, "What I remember mostly was seeing him training on the road. That's what's in my mind," he says. Kipchoge was aware that Sang had graduated from college, and that he had competed at the highest level. Those two things attracted the young Kipchoge's attention to Sang.

This morning, despite dawn's sleepiness, when the silver 12-seat Toyota Hiace, decaled with "Eliud Kipchoge INEOS 1:59:40," pulls up to the iron gate leading to Global Sports Communication training camp, it's obvious who's inside. A white KN95 mask envelops Sang's face as he slides out of the van. Thursday, April 29, 2021. 5:58 A.M. Coach is predictably punctual.

Two dozen runners at the camp prepare their Maurten bottles, shaking a portion of the powdered mix with water, a pinkish concoction of carbs and sugar essential for their bodies during this morning's workout: 30 kilometers at "easy pace" for 13 guys, including Kamworor, and 40K for six others.

The elites tote themselves to the end of the driveway at 6:15 A.M., looking like a collection of human Skittles. They're dressed in tight black shorts punctuated with bright T-shirts and running shoes, all shades of orange, purple, cobalt, and fluorescent yellow.

Sang points to a runner in a pair of bright green Nike Zoom Vaporflys. "Those shoes are okay?" he asks. While rain had ceased hours prior, evidence of the seasonal heavy downpour can be traced to milk-chocolate puddles that soaked the dirt roads throughout Kaptagat.

He looks at another runner. "You go with this group. Easy," he stresses. "You got the injection." Sang's athletes and support staff have been getting their first dose of the AstraZeneca vaccine, the only offering in Kenya at this time. While the International Olympic Committee's current regulations stipulate voluntary vaccination prior to participating in the Tokyo Olympics, Sang has elected to have everyone at camp fully vaccinated should the rules unexpectedly shift. Better to do dose 1 now so that the effects some of the athletes have been experiencing, like muscle fatigue, can pass.

Beige tape supports Kamworor's surprisingly brawny quads, peeking out from beneath skin-tight red shorts. He stands wearing black leg warmers and a white long-sleeved Nike shirt, his fingers ready to click start on his watch.

"You can go," Sang says to the group.

Sang's calmness seems typical. He insists it depends on the day. "Normally I don't even greet the athletes. When it's easy, I can say hello. But when it's real business, it's tough."

Jos Hermens uses the word *serious* to describe Sang. In all the years they've known each other, "I can't remember that we ever sat down for a coffee for an hour to bullshit," Hermens says. "We are always very serious."

A chorus of feet tapping the ground ensues as 28 men pound the tarmac, which leads to a rusty-red dirt path at the mouth of Kaptagat Forest. Sang and his four cohorts quickly pile into the van.

"This thing is modified," Sang points out. The camp had a different van for more than 10 years. "We bought this one in 2018. The one we had was much stronger. You can go anywhere. It's 4×4, but underneath we have, you know the one they use for safaris, that's what we have. We had a sunroof. I think we might even bring it back. But it's being used at a school."

A bin of Maurten bottles is tucked upfront, each athlete's name scribbled in black near the top for identification. KAMWOROR, SAMBU, KAAN, all caps. The coaches will hand out the athletes' respective bottles at five-kilometer intervals.

Seat belts remain an ignored accessory for everyone as assistant coach Richard Metto carefully steers over a bumpy road that feels like a massage for the body. The road slices parallel to crumbled brown fields with little green leaves poking out. The plant, which Kenyas call maize, is a staple to millions of people in Kenya. It is the source for ugali, a thick porridge made of cornmeal and water, bland on its own but often complemented with sukuma wiki, a dish of collard greens cooked with onions and spices. Runners here attest that they prefer to eat ugali for dinner, welcoming the slow-digesting carbs that they are convinced energize them for morning runs.

The van pulls up to the group of men, running in sync as though they'd been cloned. The seriousness and intent among the athletes is obvious. "It's an opportunity," Sang says. "In Kenya, how many people are looking for jobs?"

"I like the way they're so focused," he'll comment about the runners. Egoless, too.

Sang slides open his window.

"Iko juu zaidi!" he says. *It's too fast.* "Easy, easy, easy."

He verbally pulls the reins so his athletes don't offer themselves too intensely to the 30-kilometer workout.

Imagine if Sang had the level of support in the 1980s that he now offers his athletes instead of hearing that those who ran were fools. Imagine if he had a confidant like Metto.

"It would have done a lot," Sang laughs. "Back then, you had to think, improvise." Again he laughs, deep from the belly.

At points during the long run, Coach and his support staff pile out of the van and wait on the side of the road to dole out the bottles. The handoffs are impressively polished and take place with blink-of-an-eye quickness.

Sang is sharp, always sharp, especially his eyes. Earlier in the training session, he spotted a few runners down the road. Even at a great distance, he can determine the type of athlete. Scholarship-aiming students, he describes a pair of runners. "Or what they call in America, 'wannabes.'" Another runner is down the road. "The one on the right side . . . I think he's Indian."

The guy passes by. Sang laughs. "My eyes can see."

What he can also detect is resilience. "I see tough people when I see it," he says.

ERASING DOUBT

Daylight begins to surface just shy of 6:15 A.M., revealing a blanket of fog kissing the top of cypress trees. The soft sound of chirping birds accompanying the early hour brings another element of peace to the unspoiled lushness of the countryside. If you arrive at the end of April or the beginning of May, stripes of lilacs on both sides of the road offer a mark of direction toward Sang and his world-class associates at Global Sports Communication training camp.

A speed session is about to get underway at 8 A.M. through the robin's-egg blue gate. Tuesday mid-morning, the field is decorated with athletic clothes and shoes spread neatly across one corner and just out of range of the cow dung speckled on the grass. The track is barely separated from a handful of cattle on the other side of a wooden fence strung with thin barbed wire. When a workout isn't in session, the cows roam freely on the training ground.

At first glance, one might suspect the track isn't used much, perhaps even abandoned, due to the appearance of the rough, patchy field, dotted with small mounds of dirt and dry grass appearing desperate for rain. The track's length protrudes to 380 meters, 20 meters shy of a standard version. Mismeasured.

"When the coronavirus broke out, we had nowhere to go. All athletes were denied to enter any track," assistant coach Sugut says. "We decided to construct this. It was just open land."

It took a few months to build. Until the first few days of May 2021, the track wasn't officially marked with numbers, just a few blue hurdles in place at various distances. It wasn't until one morning, May 4, when Sang's support staff walked around with a small toothbrush dipped in white paint and wrote a few measurements—"200 meters," "600 meters," "FINISH" in all caps.

This camp is the most disciplined in Kenya, or at least that's what Olympic gold medalist Mathew Birir says. The man who outsprinted Sang for a gold medal at the 1992 Olympics later came under his wing as an athlete for a few years at the camp. Sang coached Birir in the marathon. "We used to be told, go through track and then you exit with the marathon," Birir says of the trajectory of his career. He knows firsthand just how dedicated and focused one must be to get into the training camp and also remain there. "You can be the best, but if you're not disciplined, you can be kicked out," Birir says. That, he says, is one of the most important laws of life he learned from Sang. "You cannot win if you are not disciplined," Birir says.

Sang looks on, quietly stalking various corners of the dew-covered field, his Nikes imprinting the wet grass. It's roughly 53 degrees Fahrenheit, deserving of a jacket if you're not the one moving.

Coach Metto clicks a stopwatch.

Two-time marathon world champion Abel Kirui starts the first of eight 1,600-meter repeats, dressed in tight black shorts and a maroon long-sleeved shirt. *Misuli ya mapaja na mgongo imebana sana.* He says his quads and back are tight. Kirui takes off alongside a teammate. Their feet kick up dirt as they shift from static to a high gear. This workout counts toward Kirui's preparation for the Milan Marathon on May 16, 2021.

Kirui grew up 245 kilometers south of Kaptagat in Samitoi village in Nandi County, the youngest in his family. The escarpment was like a playground; it's where he'd explore for hours at a time and run along it with a group.

During his youth he competed in 1,500 meters. He was inspired by his idol, Paul Tergat, the first Kenyan to set the world record in the marathon (he later became president of the National Olympic Committee of Kenya). Kirui would race with "Tergat" scribbled on his shirt. Kirui once said that his family's lineage of running dates back to his great-grandfather, who would chase antelope.

At 39, Kirui is a veteran in the marathon, nearly approaching what many would label as the end of his prime. He has been running since he was a young student at Samitui Primary School. His talent was "discovered" after he entered a recruitment race hosted by the Administration Police, a branch of Kenya's National Police Service. Kirui won. He joined the Administration Police thereafter and began running seriously. He holds the role of assistant superintendent of police.

Rep one. *Check.*

Metto scribbles numbers into a red notebook.

In 2006, Kirui served as a pacemaker in the Berlin Marathon, one of the world's most prestigious road races. Berlin's course, known to be flat with wide sweeping turns, monopolizes record-breaking activity. In fact, in the race's history, the marathon world record has been set in Berlin 11 times as of 2018.* Although Kirui was only meant to pace, he finished ninth overall.

Rep two. *Check.*

One year later, Kirui entered Berlin as an official competitor. His runner-up finish (2:06:51) to the legendary Ethiopian Haile Gebrselassie ranked him as the sixth-fastest marathoner ever at the time.

Rep three. *Check.*

Kirui won the silver medal in the marathon at the 2012 London Olympics. Four years later, he danced after he crossed the finish line of the Chicago Marathon in first place.

---

* Eliud Kipchoge set the men's world record for the marathon in 2018, which he again broke at the 2022 Berlin Marathon with a time of 2:01:09. It was a personal best by 30 seconds.

This was the same man who set a course record at the the Vienna Marathon in 2008. Or rather he attacked it. When Kirui entered the Amsterdam Marathon in 2014, he was considered one of the most experienced entrants in the men's elite field. He ran thinking about his grandmother, who had died the day of the race. A Seventh-Day Adventist, Kirui attends church on Saturdays, which makes him feel spiritually aligned if he races on a Sunday. His wife usually packs a Bible in his luggage. The course record and win both slipped, and Kirui moved through the finish of the Amsterdam Marathon in sixth place.

Rep four. *Check.*

Kirui spearheaded the Better Living Marathon in 2016 along with pro runners and fellow Seventh-Day Adventists Priscah Jeptoo and Amos Tirop Matui. Their intent was to educate the Adventist community and public about diseases associated with unhealthy lifestyles, like cancer and diabetes. Money raised from the marathon, held in Karura Forest in Nairobi, was to be put toward a worship and wellness center to include a gym, spa, library, and counseling center as well as a restaurant.

Kirui had trained in Iten until June 2017, when he moved to Kaptagat and lived on site at Global Sports Communication training camp. Naturally, Kipchoge was instantly his role model, whom he was eager to learn from, or rather "steal ideas from," as Kirui put it, because Kipchoge is "far smarter."

Before Kirui races, he tells himself, "I need to win today." Sometimes it happens, or else he comes close, like when he was runner-up in the Chicago Marathon in 2017.

In 2018, Kirui dropped to a seventh-place finish at the Chicago Marathon. He struggled to overcome injuries that had plagued him for two seasons. Questions surfaced as to whether Kirui had already shed his best form. He didn't race for 26 months, partly due to hip and Achilles tendon issues, and partly due to the pandemic.

It wasn't until December 2020 that he reached the starting line again at the Valencia Marathon in Spain, one of few international marathons held since the beginning of the pandemic. His seventh-place 2:05:05 performance was just barely off his personal best. He had wanted to run 2:04.

He says people have asked why he still wants to compete. Every day, he looks at Kipchoge and other training partners who are still performing. The number 2:03 is on his mind. As of May 2021, only 21 men have ever achieved that time for the marathon (and only six even faster).

Rep five. *Check.*

Kirui finally confesses that his body is betraying him. "Najikaza," he calls out to Metto. *I'm holding on.* The workout is a testing pilgrimage this morning. Sweat flicks off his face as he continues.

Rep six. *Check.*

"Nimechoka sana," he says through gritted ivory teeth, flawless and naturally straight. *I'm very tired.* "Don't think about the distance," Sang calls out. Kirui's muscles decipher the message and push onward.

"If you know yourself, then you know I'm here for a purpose. So what is my purpose?" Sang has said.

Rep seven. *Check.*

Kurui's mind attempts to mute the tension in his lower back. But his body continues to compensate. His head tilts slightly to the right as he runs, a sign of exhaustion, Eric Muthuri, one of the camp's physiotherapists, points out. He will focus on Kirui's neck during a 50-minute sports massage later.

Kirui takes off as though on autopilot. Intangible will marries desire. The workout tests his breath as his feet stomp the hard-packed dirt. This hurts. But losing hurts more.

"Very good!" Sang says. Kirui puts his hands together in prayer.

Rep eight. *Check.*

CONDITIONING

A weathered wooden floor is layered with fresh droplets of sweat raining from their necks, streaking down their backs and slipping off their chiseled calves. There is a disproportionate ratio of 19 men to one woman—their female compatriot marathoner Selly Chepyego is here six months postpartum. Collectively, they've contributed to the heavy humidity in the room, so much that it masks the front mirrors with a curtain of condensation.

It's 8:19 A.M. on a Friday in early May 2021, already one hour and change into the group's conditioning session in an orange-painted room that's nestled on a side street amid the bustle of Eldoret. The unassuming signage promoting "Mose Executive Barber Shop" at the front of Tamarind Place seems more like some sort of front for an exclusive speakeasy. Except inside the building, up a couple flights of stairs, is a small gym with a water-stained ceiling, burnt-out fluorescent lightbulb, and a few missing glass window panels.

Equipment is limited to three stability balls and four painted tires holding several weathered dumbbells; there is a pile of red and blue exercise mats near the door. When not in use, the aerobic steppers are stacked against the walls. But this morning, pairs of feet encased in a range of hot-pink, gray, and black Nikes rush on and off the boxes to the rhythmic 1-2-3-4 beat of what one runner describes as something like "Swahili Reggae." The music is mostly there as white noise. "We actually don't listen to it. We just enjoy it," says thirty-two-year-old Victor Chumo, who served as one of Kipchoge's 30 pacers for the Nike Breaking2 event in 2017.

In the middle of this mass of elite athletes is the greatest of them all, Kipchoge, hustling in nondescript dress—loose black shorts, two layered shirts, and dark exercise gloves. Just a guy who is in for the cause to bid for another Olympic marathon title in T-minus 92 days. There's little hint of his multimillion-dollar net worth, except for maybe his protruding calves, which offer a clue of extreme devotion to the sport that has made him not just one of the most recognizable runners in the world, but also one of the most highlighted athletes across all sports.

Kipchoge is out here restarting his demanding training routine after two weeks off following the NN Mission Marathon he won in April. His feet *tap-tap* the top of the step box as he holds a weight in each hand, glancing at training partner Laban Korir. One can be a seasoned elite runner and still want a little self-assurance that he's correctly performing the exercises commanded by Ben Koech, a trainer for more than two decades. Koech programs each session to focus on building full-body strength to help these runners develop more power. Both Kipchoge and Korir are members of NN Running Team, launched in April 2017.

This, the first professional running team in the world, was started by Hermens, the man who spearheads Global Sports Communication. "My dream is to grow the sport of athletics and to create a bigger fanbase by establishing more running teams and using innovation, like Wavelight and RunPuck technology," Hermens says. His idea for the NN Running Team was to help support elites with better access to coaching, nutrition, marketing, fan engagement, physiotherapy, and medical care. Backed by the NN Group, an insurance and asset management company based in the Netherlands, the NN Running Team comprises more than 60 elite runners worldwide, including some of the most accomplished marathoners, like Ethiopian Kenenisa Bekele, who held the world record in 5,000 and 10,000 meters in addition to winning three Olympic gold medals (twice in 10,000 meters and one in 5,000 meters). He is the second-fastest marathoner in history behind Kipchoge.

Actually, many of the athletes here today are resetting after recovering from the NN Mission Marathon on April 18, 2021, where Kipchoge burst back onto the scene as a leading force once more with a world-leading time of 2:04:30.

That's why the world's best runner is here grinding away during a two-hour conditioning effort that includes circuit training and abdominal work before ending on his knees in child's pose, a resting position—and fundamental yoga pose—that stabilizes the spine and decompresses the back. It's a sliver of the prescription that keeps him at the top of his game at age 36.

Chumo bought into the plan, too, when he joined Global Sports Communication training camp in 2017, after he worked in the engineers unit of the Kenya Defence Forces, where he was tasked with disarming bombs. He quit after five years to pursue running full time. In 2016, Chumo had targeted a spot on Kenya's Olympic team for Rio, but he missed qualifying for the 5,000 meters after he finished a disappointing 11th at the country's Olympic Trials.

When Chumo switched from famed Italian running coach Renato Canova to train under Sang, he worked to polish his pacemaker role for the Nike Breaking2 project in Italy, then later as a pacer for Kipchoge for the INEOS 1:59 Challenge, which took place in October 2019 in Vienna, Austria. Of course, the world is familiar with that end result, an epic achievement that proved the impossible was actually possible—under the guise of careful orchestration and involving guys like Chumo.

Chumo is grateful for what the experience taught him about running, racing, and being a selfless leader. Now Chumo has turned his attention to his own results: his half marathon personal best of 59:58 just cracks the top 200 of all time (as of May 2021). He intends to make his marathon debut hopefully a few months from now, with the goal of running 2:05.

So he has to be here, inside this muggy room, edging toward the end of the conditioning session with a series of fire hydrants, an exercise that singes the glutes. Midway through 10 reps, some runners make eye contact and quietly laugh, but then switch to gritting their teeth. The burn is too real. This workout, some of the guys say afterward, feels harder than running.

A CUT ABOVE

A rooster crows.

A young Kenyan boy rides a rusty bike across a flat dirt road.

A police officer in a fluorescent green vest stands on a corner wearing a face mask.

Leaves of maize lay still.

A cow nuzzles his nose against a telephone pole, relieving an itch.

A boy dressed in a coral T-shirt and khaki pants swings a hoe into crumbled dirt.

A woman sits on the side of the road gently rotating corn over a small pile of charcoal.

A white van transports green bananas on its roof.

A toddler in a black shirt and pants sits on the ground gently scooping dirt.

Her back is turned to the action on a nondescript dirt field in Kapsabet, the capital of Nandi County, approximately 40 kilometers southwest of Eldoret. The child pays no attention to the significance unfolding behind her on Saturday, May 22, 2021. Ordinary life moves in parallel to an alternative reality taking shape at the Athletics Kenya Central Rift Under-20 pre-trials. Nandi is referred to as the "Source of Champions." Drive through the blue arch at the border and one will even see the words hoisted above the road. The sign is hard to miss. There are signs all around, actually.

Runners are peppered throughout the area, as though built into the environment. Another hint is on this field.

A crowd forms a *u* shape at the south end of the dirt track, chalked with eight white lanes that encircle a patchy grass field. In the crowd, some men are dressed in collared button-down shirts and trousers. Blue face masks showcase who is choosing to be more responsible among the masses.

Cameramen move about as fans of the youth eagerly peer at what could very well be the future of Kenyan athletics. Raw talent, as Sang describes. The pre-trials—a stepping stone to the World Athletics Under-20 Championships—skims a handful of the best amateur runners, a dress rehearsal of sorts for these boys and girls, who will move on to a national meet at Nyayo National Stadium that will take place during the first two days of July.

The grassy parking lot pockets the Toyota Hiace—the same vehicle that only days ago tracked Kipchoge and his training partners for 40 kilometers, a run that nearly equaled the distance of a marathon. Coach Metto stalks the field dressed in orange Nikes, blue jeans, and a white short-sleeved collared shirt. He's here watching over a few juniors from the training camp.

Somewhere in the mix is the camp's 19-year-old Jackline Chepkoech, who is already dressed in her race kit: a green and black dotted racerback and black Adidas shorts. Her head is stripped of any feminine touch. No ponytail. No braids. Just close-cropped hair. Chepkoech's soft smile disappears when she's training or competing, but she wears it humbly off the track. It buries a painful upbringing. Shedding this previous existence, she had worked to relearn how to trust.

Chepkoech grew up in Olenguruone in Nakuru County. She started running at age 11 while in primary school. She dropped out of Winners Girls High School in 2019, aged 16, due to lack of school fees. Then, Chepkoech opted to train at the Keringet Athletics Training Camp.

When the hand of fate scooped her into Global Sports Communication training camp, the junior athlete adopted an unfamiliar workload in pursuit of revising her future. "The people around you determine what you become, what you think," Sang has said. And one becomes a reflection of that environment, he adds.

Chepkoech is in a space to thrive. The junior, by the way, is mentored at the camp by one of her idols, Olympic silver medal steeplechaser Hyvin Kiyeng. Chepkoech is learning the ropes of this world. As she does, she continues to emerge as a champion brimming with promise—and as the media aptly describes, a woman that "dominates." Reporters call her young, unequivocally unaware of her ripened mentality from having to grow up quickly. Had they known of her past, perhaps *young* would be replaced by *mature*. She is chasing a certain future. Chepkoech wants to break the women's steeplechase world record held by Kenyan Beatrice Chepkoech (of no relation). The younger Chepkoech is aiming to compete in the 2024 Summer Olympics in Paris.

That is her plan.

Chepkoech's feet are encased in black Adidas spikes with purple trim. Some women who competed earlier were barefoot in skirts. One had a blue face mask dangling from her pocket. Chepkoech's shirt tag sticks out as she walks toward the start for the steeplechase. Wearing chest number 115, her race bib, the young woman aligns the start at 1:03 P.M., ready to prove that her lean legs carry substance.

"Silence for the start," the announcer calls out. The sound of a starting pistol snaps into the air.

Left foot forward, Chepkoech begins her elongated sprint, moving with equal parts grace and power. The way she picks up her feet with ease as she leaps over a black and white wooden hurdle, one wonders: is she even racing or simply going through the motions as she escapes her competitors? A gap spreads between Chepkoech and the other young women. They already can't keep up with her just one lap of seven and a half into the race.

Children stand next to adults, hands folded behind their backs. The sun is high in the sky, and therefore shadows are shorter. The 74-degree temperature envelops this particular moment of little eyes peering at the eight lanes as the sound of track spikes munch on the dirt. Lanky legs move with purpose, attempting the plan each one believes God has for them. Chepkoech maintains her rhythm. Child's play, it seems. But this race is a necessary sliver of her Saturday. A necessary step to nationals.

Her plan.

"You finish with a burst. You finish with a torso!" The announcer, referred to as "Mr. Melly," has an enthusiasm that seems to stick in the air.

Chepkoech's rhythm has yet to escape her. She keeps moving, her stride just as wide as when she started the race. She is inching closer to her plan. Two laps to go. For her, at least. Chepkoech continues to define herself in front of the crowd of at least 200, who've stayed around in support of this second to last event of the day. Opposite arm, opposite leg. Opposite arm, opposite leg. Each leg kicks up high behind her. No sign of fatigue. She runs as though she's more seasoned than she actually is.

1:14 P.M., her feet meet victory.

Her plan will continue.

MADARAKA DAY

June 1, 2021, Tuesday, was business as usual. A track session. A red notebook to record splits of the thread of speed swirling around at the training camp. Some of the athletes read over the morning workout, which includes 5 × 2,000 meters and 5 × 1,000 meters.

At 9:25 A.M., Kipchoge, dressed in a light yellow shirt and black shorts, takes off sprinting clockwise around the track behind two dozen men. His mouth curves slightly upward, as though he is holding back a smile. A vein protrudes from his left temple.

The men run single file in the inner lane, the most weathered one on the track. Sweat rains quickly from their bodies, glittering down their foreheads. Is it the wind or their quickness that is making their shirts flap? Victor Chumo laps the track alone, glancing at his watch. He is nursing a strained groin. It will be fine in a month, he says later.

The field is dry. It hasn't rained for days, but the sky is telling. A local will say that rain follows the full and new moon phases. Showers will come within the next two weeks.

By 11 A.M., there's an audible shift on the track. Spikes dig into the dirt. The 800-meter specialist Wycliffe Kinyamal runs counterclockwise to warm up before he begins his speed session. Faith Kipyegon is out here, too, slightly increasing the ratio of women—there are fewer than five at the moment. Just days ago on May 28, Kipyegon competed in a Diamond League meet in Doha, Qatar, where she won the women's 800 meters. Dressed in a hot-pink shirt and black shorts, Kipyegon begins the first portion of her workout, 2 × 2,000 meters. She is preparing for the upcoming Olympic Trials that will take place mid-June.

Coach Sang stands on the field wearing a white polo shirt and black slacks, the outfit capped with a white hat. Even outside, in the fresh country air, he is shielding himself with a blue face mask. His hands are folded behind him as he looks on at the details of the morning—the men and women of this camp he is readying for brighter futures.

Today is the 58th anniversary of Madaraka Day, Kenya's national holiday to commemorate when the country attained self-rule from Britain. That day, June 1, 1963, Jomo Kenyatta was sworn in as the prime minister of Kenya (it wasn't until December 12, 1963, though, when Kenya declared its independence).

Not long after the track session, one athlete fills two blue plastic buckets with water. He takes a bar of soap and begins scrubbing his running clothes. Rinse. Repeat. He will hang them to dry under the warm sun. Next he will wash his training shoes. He is not alone in the care he takes for his belongings. Every athlete will repeat this weekly ritual, Kipchoge included. Life at camp.

When he is done, he will join other members of camp who are sitting around in the sun, their eyes glued to their smartphones as they watch and listen intently as President Uhuru Kenyatta—His Excellency, as he's referred to—offers a televised speech to the Republic of Kenya in honor of Madaraka Day. The speech, delivered from Jomo Kenyatta International Stadium in Kisumu, is a version of the US's State of the Union address, in which the president provides a yearly message about the current condition of the nation.

Just four years ago, President Kenyatta spoke of waiving import duty so that milk and other foods would remain affordable, he spoke of livestock insurance to protect pastoralist communities from losses to drought, he revealed a plan in the works for the revival of Kenya's coffee sector, and he spoke of Kenya as having one of the largest economies in Africa.

But President Kenyatta also spoke of the need for jobs. "We must find jobs for all our sons and daughters who have met their part of the bargain by diligently going to school," he said in his speech. He had told the people, "My government understands that every corner of Kenya matters; every Kenyan deserves basic services. I am proud today to report that in the last four years, we have added more than 2 million homes to the electricity grid." That included some 23,000 primary schools across the country that would be provided electricity.*

President Kenyatta addressed a desire for a "Kenya whose people won't have to attend weekly harambees or spend family savings to send relatives and friends abroad for modern health services."

President Kenyatta's address is a bit different in 2021. He talks about the country's annual worth of 10.3 trillion shillings (some 85 billion USD). Economic acceleration, sending more national revenue to counties, "Big Push Investments"—laying the ground for economic takeoff, he says. He speaks of infrastructure projects—reviving the railways, building roads. The road is not the dream. The dream is what roads can do for the country, he explains.

The athletes remain silent as they absorb more words from His Excellency about the economics of decisions, about an upgraded health care infrastructure. President Kenyatta gets specific, pointing out the 54 renal units with 360 state-of-the-art dialysis machines distributed among all 47 counties in the country. He ends with more words about the economics of decisions. There's a consequence for every choice one makes.

---

* After Faith Kipyegon won gold at the 2016 Rio Olympics, the village where her parents live, Keringet, was installed with electricity for the first time, as part of the Kenyan government's three-year initiative called the Last Mile Connectivity Program, which aims to affordably connect Kenyan households to the national network grid.

As the president ends his speech, clean pairs of Nike VaporFly shoes that were hand-washed in a blue plastic bucket of water with bar soap are laid on a roof to dry. Tomorrow, the shoes will be covered with dirt. Then the shoes will be scrubbed again so clean they will appear like new. The athlete will do it again and again and again, until the shoes are too worn out to support another mile. When the shoes are replaced, the fresh pair will be handled with care, hand-washed often. By choice.

THE LION'S DEN

I n Kenyan context, you really never plan as an individual that I'm competing in this Olympics, or let me see what I can do in the next Olympics," Sang says. Just like in the US, Kenya's team for track and field is not determined until one month before the Olympics, when the country holds its trials. The trials in Kenya are in many ways more pressure-filled than the Games themselves.

Kenya's Olympic Trials are set to take place from June 17–19, 2021, at the Moi International Sports Centre in Kasarani, 12 kilometers from the country's capital. It is the largest stadium in Kenya, originally built in 1987 to host the All-Africa Games, an international track and field competition held every four years, featuring athletes from the nations of Africa.

Unlike in previous Olympic Trials, when the 60,000-seat venue would be bloated with roaring spectators there to watch the national sport of athletics the way Americans are dedicated to professional football and basketball, this edition is reflective of current affairs—that is, necessarily cautious amid a worldwide pandemic. Therefore, the stadium is mostly vacant sans a handful of coaches permitted into the stands—Sang included, of course.

Kamworor is here. He is ripe and ready to make his second Olympic team.

Back in 1992, when Sang was on the starting line at the trials, he was part of what Brother Colm described as "the greatest collection of steeplechasers that the world has ever seen." Twelve, to be precise. Former world record holder Peter Koech. Reigning Olympic champion Julius Kariuki, who was still a collegiate athlete when he won the gold in 1988 in Seoul. World record holder and world champion Moses Kiptanui. And Mathew Birir, then 20, a young gun among giants. "You name it. The Who's Who lined up for that steeplechase. Incredible," says Brother Colm, who watched the event in person. The race was wide open and expectedly suspenseful.

Kenya has amassed more than 20 Olympic medals in the men's steeplechase, gold for every Games from 1968 to 2016 (with the exception of 1976 and 1980, when Kenya did not participate). "The steeplechase is a very tough event. You have to be a hurdler. You have to be a sprinter. You have to be a long-distance runner. All the things," Birir says.

"That race stands out for me more than the Olympic final. More!" Brother Colm says. "I could appreciate the caliber of athletes." Reputation or status or success meant little on the starting line, as the men stood equally ready to make the team. Birir had to run the fastest time ever at altitude to win, Brother Colm recalls. Sang was second. "I was lucky I made the team," he says. "Up against tough guys, guys who had run world records!" His tone is one of successive exclamation points.

Not only did Sang make his second Olympic team, but he was also appointed captain for the entire Kenya Olympic team, and he served as the flag bearer for his country.

Being considered a leader offered Sang another layer of awareness. "You understand from sitting in management meetings that the priority is medals. Gold. Not silver. Not bronze," Sang says. Gold is everything. "That's how Kenyans think."

That was then, and this is now. Gold is still important. And the Olympic Trials is still the lion's den, as it is not unusual for most of the entrants to be capable of making the Kenyan Olympic team. But only three will. If ever there is an occasion, apart from the actual Olympics, when one must be on the top of one's game, *this is it*. One must mentally bow to that truth. Accept the pressure. One is free to either internalize it or find a way to appreciate it. The mark of a champion is how well he can play with it. Use it. Burn it off.

Such a scenario isn't limited to Kenya's athletics. Such a scenario is a natural part of sports. But in Kenya, the scenario is inflated. For runners here, so many of whom are athletically blessed and filled with aspiration, racing then becomes an aggressive game of Darwinism.

Talent is limited without drive. The motivation. The *Why*. Why do you accept that the labyrinth to the top will be full of discomfort, full of pain? Why do you accept that there must be some sort of sacrifice?

The *Why* plucks your body out of bed before light cracks the darkness of the day. The *Why* is the reason you endure achy muscles, exhaustion, cycles of highs and lows. The *Why* is wanting to be somebody. The *Why* is for the glory. The *Why* is also for a life-changing opportunity.

June 18, 2021, Kamworor slips on his racing kit, a blue singlet with funky green and blue geometric lines and matching short shorts. His tank top carries race bib 234. Before he steps to the starting line, Kamworor has a word with his friend, training partner, and mentor, Kipchoge. "Let's go to Tokyo together," Kipchoge tells him. He had advised Kamworor, "Trust the system. Trust that you are the best one in the field." Believe in yourself.

Kamworor stands in lane 3, one man among 32 other entrants. Thirty-two other entrants that want to be among the top three, just like him. Well, the top two. The third spot is the decision of Athletics Kenya, the country's governing body for athletics. These men understand that, and perhaps, another stake. Kenya owns only one Olympic gold medal in the event, and it was earned long before any of them were born. Naftali Temu, 1968 Mexico City Olympics. Kenya's reputation thereafter in the men's 10,000 meters: bronze, bronze, silver, silver,

silver, bronze, silver. In that order. The Tokyo Olympics will be another chance to change the statistic. But first, Kamworor must close out the race before that opportunity can be issued.

Twenty-five laps to go for a spot on the team.

The men start the race by running in a compact string. Four minutes later, Kamworor, in fifth position, is passed. He doesn't accept the move. Clearly. So he accelerates to third. How strange it must be to run with so much intent, so much at stake, to a quiet backdrop, as though this is some sort of dress rehearsal. Except, *this is it*.

By minute 5, Kamworor is second. The compact string begins to loosen. Contenders versus remnants. His stride is smooth, elongated. This is the day he's been waiting for. All those heartbeats on his stationary bike. All those heartbeats on the dirt paths, up hills, at high altitude. All those heartbeats to make his vision become real.

As Kamworor runs, he continues to trail the young Rhonex Kipruto. Halfway through the race, the competition escalates. Kamworor is among the top three as the pack separates from the rest of the field. The chasers were ten, then seven, then six, now just a trio. Kamworor takes the lead. An announcer roars his name, and the sound reverberates throughout the stadium. He signals to the two men behind him to go in front. It's their turn. He is not going to be the rabbit. Work together. Work together until it's time to untether. They do for a moment.

And then there are two. Kamworor retakes the lead. *This is it.*

The bell lap. The last go round. Kamworor is in position 1, followed closely by Kipruto. Two hundred meters remain. And then there is one.

Kamworor salutes with his right hand as he continues to sprint. One hundred meters remain. He continues to sprint. And continues to sprint until he runs through the finish line. A wide smile immediately spreads across his face. The top spot, 27:01.06—27 seconds ahead of the Olympic standard. He punches the air.

This is the *Why*.

mtaka cha uvunguni sharti ainame

without labor, nothing prospers

CHASING

Usually, it's the same sliver of time, 5:50 , when the world's eye peels open with burnt-orange and peachy blushes of light. If one could taste pre-sunrise, it would be delicate and sweet, something like fresh honeycomb.

And at this hour, her feet have already touched the floor as she readies herself to reel in another part of her dream.

Every day she wakes up to honor the thought. Her psyche persuades her body to run for a minute more, a kilometer longer, leaving her pooled in sweat.

She has to do it again. Again. Again. And again.

It's as though her muscles, lungs, and heart are pumping through a long-form equation. It all brings her just a fraction closer to her dream. But closer still.

It can make her muscles swollen and tired from her mind constantly convincing her that she can do it—make her dream real.

At 5-foot-2 and barely 100 pounds, Faith Kipyegon hardly seems threatening, especially with a glowing smile often stamped across her face. It's the kind of expression that is a genuine degree of happy, free of stress that only Kenyan sunshine, clean air, and the quiet surroundings of Kaptagat can produce.

She is 27. Young, yet seasoned in the sport. Or rather, blossomed. If one didn't know better, Kipyegon could seem like just a woman who runs a lot. But if one knows better, Kipyegon is not just a woman who runs a lot. She has been competitive for more than a decade. The top of the podium is a familiar spot. In that sense, she is unassumingly threatening simply when her feet are positioned behind the starting line. A petite package of speed and endurance. Is it still considered competitive if you usually win? And competitive to whom? *Oneself?*

Kipyegon's cocoa-colored eyes reflect that this woman has a laser focus only elite athletes working to be the best have. She doesn't stray from her lane. Her day-to-day rhythm is necessarily monotonous. Wake up. Run. Eat. Rest. Run. Eat. Rest. Lights off. Another day, another week, another month, another year. Is this more taxing for the body or the mind? Regardless, this focus is what allows one to understand that winning—at the highest level—is not a mirage. It is a real vision. Very real.

If one can make it to this exceptionally elite phase, there are still so many points to reach before the crescendo. The climax for Kipyegon, of course, is the Olympic final on August 6, 2021. But prior to that date is a prerequisite on June 17, 2021, the day of Kenya's Olympic Trials for the women's 1,500 meters. The first two athletes across the finish line earn an automatic spot to the Olympic Games in Tokyo as long as each achieves the qualifying standard.

The appointment takes place on a Thursday. Kipyegon is here, ready to quietly show up for herself and test the relationship between her psyche and her body. The two must harmoniously connect. Few can master the delicate balance. She can.

Her first name, printed in white block letters on the race bib pinned to her sleeveless jersey, seems symbolic. Her name is Faith, and she has it, too. Red nails, painted on all but her fourth fingers, which are coated in sky-blue polish, adds a feminine touch to this serious business endeavor—making her third consecutive Olympic team. This woman is an athlete. This athlete is a woman. One can be both. She is *both*.

Usually Kipyegon races in a cropped tank. But today, her jersey is long enough to cover the stretch marks that streak across her abdomen, a subtle tip-off that this athlete is also a mother. And this mother is an athlete. One can be both. She is *both*.

The gun snaps. Her legs go. Go. Go. And go, rushing to meet her fate. This is a moment very few will ever understand. Very, very few.

Four laps explain the next direction. Will she or won't she be in the top two among 13 total competitors? As she runs, at the front, the answer quickly appears. The clock is like a digital heartbeat, pumping out numbers as Kipyegon pumps out her response to the question *Does she still have it?*

Yes, in fact, she does. The lead from the gun. The lead on the bell lap ahead of Winny Chebet. The lead to the tape. She has it in 4:02.10. She has the win—and a place on Kenya's Olympic team.

The media described her race as an "easy" victory. *Easy*, the operative word.

Her body and her psyche have passed the first big test. The other big test will come weeks from now, thousands of miles away from home soil, on another continent. Will she be ready when the crescendo arrives?

Will she still have it?

FRACTURED

In the dream, he gets on the plane bound for the Tokyo Olympics outfitted in black, red, and green. Black to represent the people of the Republic of Kenya, red to honor Kenya's fight for independence, and green to symbolize the country's lush landscape. These are the colors that make up Kenya's flag, along with the Maasai shield, a mark of defense, stamped in the center, perpendicular to two lines in white, the color of peace.

Kamworor has the honor of wearing the colors in the dream as he represents his country at the Olympics, just as Sang did twice in 1988 and 1992, before Kamworor was born. The dream continues with Kamworor arriving in the Japanese capital for a different version of the Olympics, this one thick with health restrictions and protocols, rather than a cohesive mix of athletes curiously crossing paths in the Olympic Village, as Sang experienced when he was a competitive athlete.

Though these Games are operated in an unprecedented way, at least the Olympics are still occurring, and therefore Kamworor has the opportunity to compete in the men's 10,000-meter final on July 30, 2021. Friday at 7 P.M. is to be a moment to show his revival, not just after mending his body post-accident, but also from five years ago in Rio, when Kamworor competed in his first Olympics and finished 11th in the 10,000 meters.

The years and the accident have matured Kamworor compared to his younger self in Rio. Now he is on the starting line once again. And in the dream, he runs with his perfectly cadenced, elongated, and graceful stride. His face is stoic, his eyes intensely staring ahead. It all goes accordingly, as though his mind and body have an arrangement. Just like what happened at Kenya's Olympic Trials, when he won. In the dream, he leads the Olympic race in lane one. His mind carries a vision he's had since he was a teenager, that one day he would become a champion on the highest stage. His legs usher that hope. This is how it's supposed to unfold.

But the dream stops abruptly.

Kamworor wakes up one day in July to news. His right foot. Metatarsal fracture. "I think it happened during speed work. I did a lot of training, a lot of speed, and then there was a lot of pressure on the metatarsal," he deduces. Four weeks of rest are in order.

In the dream he was healthy. His body wasn't being punished for his necessary devotion to the sport. The news comes at a time when the sky cries in Kenya. Heavy rains in July seem to mirror Kamworor's disappointment. This isn't how it's supposed to unfold. Dreams aren't supposed to make your heart break.

"I must have an Olympic medal from the track," he said months earlier in the spring. "Any medal before I fully move to the marathon . . . Whatever comes with it always benefits the family, the community, society."

It's like a ripple effect, Kipchoge explains. "The community will treat themselves like they are gold medalists. People will start to think positively and get motivation. 'This guy from this village can win, and he's just from here.'" The mentality then becomes *We can also excel in other things*. "It makes people want to work harder in life," Kipchoge says.

Kamworor had received his second dose of the AstraZeneca vaccine at the end of June along with a COVID-19 vaccination certificate. Logistically, he was ready. Mentally, he was ready. He was conditioned for Japan, even despite the ongoing downpours interfering with his preparation for the Olympics. The rains kept making it difficult to train, he said. More runs on tarmac than he preferred, but he was managing.

Prior to the news, one could think the narrative was a sort of suspenseful fairy tale: elite athlete experiences terrible accident; emergency room, surgery, stitches; crutches, one step, followed by one step more; walking, *slowly*; then running, *slowly*; then running fast, then faster, and finally ascending to the rarefied rank of elite. He is gifted with time to prepare for the Olympics. He managed to inch his way back to the top by winning Kenya's trials, resulting in a coveted spot on the Olympic team.

"With a lot of focus, you can do it. Despite the challenges you are going through or that your country is going through, that everyone is going through, it cannot hinder you from achieving your target and from achieving your goals," Kamworor said a week and a half before he was supposed to leave for the Tokyo Olympics.

Supposed to.

Sometimes the fairy tale seems too good to be true, because it is. Perhaps in a parallel universe, the narrative meets a more favorable fate. But in this dimension, it doesn't. The narrative is suspended. *Ready to compete.* Or at least, those were the words he used nine days before he announced he was pulling out of the Olympics. It was not in his best interest to lap the track in Tokyo twenty-five times with only featherweight spikes to bear the weight of his swift, bounding strides.

Why did the goal have to be involuntarily seized? He is forced to sit with the sentiment of disappointment. "I had no choice. It was beyond my control. I had to accept," he says.

So instead of stepping onto the plane en route to Japan, like his campmates Kipchoge and Kipyegon, Kamworor will no longer share in the privilege of putting on Kenya's striking black, red, and green uniforms for the Olympics and contribute to a reputation of being from a country that produces some of the most outstanding talents in running the world has ever seen. Kipchoge described the news as a huge shock. "In my mind I was actually envisioning the gold that Geoffrey would win in the Olympics," he said.

July 30, what would have been Kamworor's Olympic moment he will instead watch on a screen thousands of miles away on a different continent. It was a mental cut, bandaged by the words "I will come back stronger."

What if he had been healthy? What if he had competed in Tokyo? Would the dream of a medal, a gold one, come true?

What if.

"Injuries are part of the sport. You never know what will happen during training," he says. "If you don't accept the situation, you might not have enough confidence to bounce back."

He was so close. So close. What will happen to him now? Where does he go from here?

Forward, he says. Reach for the next branch.

TOKYO FROM 1964 TO ~~2020~~ 2021

A white goatee traces Wilson Kiprugut's chin. His lips move gingerly, just like his feet; these days the 83-year-old relies on a cane to maintain balance. Gone is the short black hair of his youth. His dark brown eyes were wider back then. His vision continues to fade as does his ability to hold a pen, but his mind hasn't slipped. When Kiprugut digs 57 years back into his memory, his voice is soft and light as he recalls his experience competing in the 1964 Tokyo Olympics.

He remembers the way he stood in the tunnel joking as he waited to be called to the starting line with seven other men for the 800-meter final; the crowd inside the National Stadium erupting with chants of "Kenya! Kenya!" and the feeling of soft ribbon bearing a small weight dangling from his neck as he stood on the podium flashing a brilliant smile.

Kenya, newly independent from Britain for just 10 months, had sent Kiprugut, a member of the King's African Rifles (the predecessor to what is now the Kenya Defence Forces), to compete in the 800 meters. This was Kenya's third time participating in an Olympic Games. For two occasions prior, the country had closed its participation without the honor of standing on a podium. Kiprugut was prepared to amend the story of the medal-less nation.

He had come a long way from where he was born and raised in Kericho, located at the edge of the Mau Forest, on the western escarpment of the Great Rift Valley. The area is lush with wide fields of emerald maize crops and mostly recognized for its immaculate bushes of tea plantations, so picturesque they look unreal.

Kiprugut, who grew up as one of seven siblings, got his start in running as a student at Kaptebeswet Primary School and continued athletics at Sitotwet Intermediate School. Running, though, was something he mostly did out of necessity—five kilometers one way in the morning to school; another round home in the afternoon. His talent was scouted by the King's African Rifles when he competed in the 800 meters at the 1958 East African Championship in Tanzania.

Thereafter, Kiprugut joined the military, training as a track athlete alongside other members of the army while he worked his way up to the rank of senior sergeant. By 1962, Kiprugut was primed for his intercontinental racing debut at the British Empire and Commonwealth Games, held in Perth, Australia, as a member of Kenya's 4 × 440 yards relay team, which placed fifth.

Kiprugut matured his athleticism with training ideas borrowed from competitors who became friends. He complemented his preparation with guidance from fellow officers. When Kiprugut earned the opportunity to compete in Tokyo, he said, "I knew I would make something good." His intuition and confidence were thick, even before he stepped inside the airplane in Nairobi, bound for Japan.

The ease of qualifying out of heat one—he clocked 1:47:8—inched him closer to proving it. He made it through the semi-finals even faster, 1:46:01, earning a spot in the final. Though Kiprugut had never raced against any of the seven other men who had qualified out of their respective heats—six first rounds and three semi-finals—he felt well prepared when he woke up on October 16, 1964, the day of the final. Kiprugut remembers thinking, "I have two legs and they have two legs. I can make it."

The race, one of seven men's track events at these Games, took place at Tokyo's National Stadium. Kiprugut stood wearing bib 386 alongside defending champion Peter Snell of New Zealand, Canadian Bill Crothers, and Jamaican George Kerr.

The men took off from a crouched starting position in front of boisterous spectators, legs immediately darting full throttle. Kiprugut led the pack. Race favorite Snell's plan to pull ahead was thwarted when he became boxed in along the rail.

By lap 2, Snell had found his way through to the front. Kiprugut remembers Kerr's elbow bumping his chest. Then Kerr stumbled, slightly disrupting Kiprugut's rhythm. Kiprugut recovered from the blunder, though, and continued, shifting gears.

On the back straight of lap 2, Snell unleashed his signature powerful stride (so aggressive, in fact, that teammate John Davies had witnessed his feet tearing into the cinder track five days later, when Snell won gold in the 1,500 meters). Snell's burst of speed propelled him three meters out of range from Crothers and Kiprugut, who ran second and third, respectively. Kiprugut recalls hearing the crowd erupt with cheers, shouting for his country. His effort pulled him through the homestretch as he dipped across the finish line with a time of 1:45.9—third place. Suddenly Kenya's unmarked Olympic history on a podium was no longer blank. Bronze was a victory.

Kiprugut laughed as he stood on the podium, raising his hands above his head in a folded prayer as the Kenyan flag was hoisted for the first time.

By the time Kiprugut landed at Embakasi Airport (now Jomo Kenyatta International Airport) in Nairobi, he was carried by a dozen Indians, members of Kenya's Olympic field hockey team, who toted their hero from the plane to the airport lounge, then to the bus—every one of them dressed in a suit jacket, collared shirt, tie, and slacks. Kiprugut grinned as he was lifted onto their shoulders.

Since Kiprugut's podium finish, Kenya has gone on to amass more than 100 medals at successive Olympics—including Kiprugut's silver earned four years later in Mexico City—the most of any country in Africa. When Sang arrives in Japan for the Tokyo Olympics, it will mark 33 years since he, too, first competed in the Games. Sang, of course, has contributed to Kenya's medal tally, in the silver category. And his athletes have as well over the years. At the Tokyo Olympics, they aim to continue to do so.

On a warm Friday evening, July 23, 2021, in Tokyo, athletes representing 206 delegations parade at the opening ceremony for the XXXII Olympiad. The city is in a state of emergency and will continue to be throughout the Olympics.

Though a year later than originally scheduled, the Games are branded as Tokyo 2020 and are the most expensive Summer Olympics to date, according to a report by the *Washington Post*, which notes that Japanese government auditors estimate at least $25 billion (for comparison, the tab for the 2016 Rio Games was $13.7 billion, and approximately $15 billion for the 2012 London Olympics as reported by *Forbes*).

Tokyo is the only city in Asia to stage the Summer Olympics twice.* The first time in 1964, Japan had welcomed more than 5,000 athletes from nearly 100 countries. Nineteen-year-old collegiate runner Yoshinori Sakai served as the final torch bearer. Sakai, born August 6, 1945, the day the atomic bomb exploded in Hiroshima, was chosen in homage to the victims. When he lit the cauldron on October 10, 1964, it was considered one of the most dramatic moments of those Games, not only signaling the official start of the 18th Olympiad, but also a call for world peace.

This version of the Tokyo Games is brimming with tension. "Tokyo Olympics should not be held in 2021 under COVID's long shadow," a

---

* Beijing hosted the Olympics Games twice, but once for the Summer Games and once for the Winter Games.

headline in *The San Francisco Chronicle*; "Japan nurses voice anger at call to volunteer for Tokyo Olympics amid Covid crisis," appeared in *The Guardian*. At the end of April 2021, organizers stated that all athletes will be tested daily for COVID-19 (instead of the previously specified every four days) as part of countermeasures in the effort to minimize the spread and move competitions forward.

Organizers of the Tokyo Olympics are also faced with the issue of heat. During the summer, the average daily temperature warms to 82 degrees Fahrenheit, and it can tip upward of 88 degrees in July and August. Those months are complemented with humidity ranging from 73 to 77 percent. Too much moisture in the air also makes it more challenging for the body to cool itself. The heat expected during the Tokyo Games swayed the International Olympic Committee to announce in October 2019 that the women's and men's marathons will take place 500 miles north of Tokyo in Sapporo, where temperatures are usually 10 to 12 degrees cooler than in the country's capital in early August.

The COVID-19 countermeasures and mandates for the Summer Games are outlined in playbooks, which list detailed protocol such as: meals must be eaten two meters away from others; no use of public transit during the first 14 days after arrival; mandatory facemasks, and athletes must be tested daily. It is not mandatory that each athlete be vaccinated in order to compete. International and domestic spectators are banned from attending Olympic stadiums and arenas in Tokyo to watch the Games as they unfold from July 23 to August 8.

The crowd is a large part of what makes the atmosphere at the Olympics. Just imagine preparing for the apex of your career and having to present yourself to mostly vacant seats. This wasn't how it's supposed to go. But this is how it's going.

Of the 11,420 athletes participating in the Tokyo Olympics, Kenya has sent 85, 38 of whom represent track and field and the marathon—Kipyegon and Kipchoge among them, along with other members of the training camp. Hyvin Kiyeng will compete in the women's steeplechase, and Rodgers Kwemoi will take on the men's 10,000 meters.

The view from the top of the National Stadium in the Shinjuku district of Tokyo looks like a pixelated monochrome image of Tetris. Seats, capacity up to 68,000, are mostly empty, though under normal circumstances—less a non-pandemic reality—the space would be brimming with people, eyes eager to catch a glimpse of the world's best track athletes in action. Such irony that in the world's largest metropolitan city, the prized venue that is the grand stage for track and field events of the Olympic Games is so unnaturally hushed.

The women's 1,500 meters final seems less real without a boisterous soundtrack to rally competitors here from all over the world and who have fought for their place on the starting line. The preliminary round of the women's 1,500 meters was held on August 2 and included 45 entrants split among three heats. The semi-finals took place two days later, on August 4, featuring 26 entrants. And now 13 women are facing off in the final.

Racing is like life, challenge after challenge. And this next critical challenge is a matchup between Kipyegon and double world champion Sifan Hassan, the Ethiopian-born runner who is representing the Netherlands in an unprecedented triple: 1,500, 5,000, and 10,000 meters. British record holder Laura Muir, who finished seventh in this event five years ago at the Rio Olympics and fifth at the 2019 World Championships, is also on the line, "good enough to get the bronze," a commentator points out. But bronze is a different shade of winning.

Each woman is introduced over a speaker. Kipyegon is the last competitor to be called, right before the newly crowned 5,000-meter Olympic gold medalist Hassan walks through the tunnel and to the starting line. They've exchanged equivalent retaliation over the years. Hassan had beaten Kipyegon at the 2019 World Championships in Doha. Kipyegon outpaced Hassan in their last race before these Olympics, at a Diamond League meet in Monaco. Kipyegon's world-leading time, 3:51.07, also set the Kenyan national record. Two once-in-a-generation athletes.

The number 10 is stickered on each side of Kipyegon's hips. She stands in lane 7, bouncing up and down next to Hassan. The final is effectively positioned as two races in one. Kipyegon and Hassan, "those two" as they're described—and everyone else versus everyone else.

Kipyegon crosses herself, acknowledging God's presence. May this woman who is a mother, this mother who is an athlete, be protected as she sets off to prove that she is the best of the best in the women's 1,500 meters, one of the blue-ribbon events of the Olympics.

This is a moment that very few can relate to. A defending Olympic champion about to run through the gauntlet of competitors that wish to dethrone her as she tries to prove that *she still has it*.

Click.

A snapping sound of the starting pistol signals *Go! Now!* And they do. Those two—Kipyegon and Hassan—are in the back just for a moment before sprinting to the front.

Lap 1, Hassan-Kipyegon. By a half stride. The reigning world champion Hassan wants to dictate the race early.

Lap 2, Hassan-Kipyegon, 2:07 at the half.

Wait for it.

The string of competitors separate. Hassan, Kipyegon, and Muir, in a pack, in that order. It's sticky and mid-80 degrees Farenheit. They don't show any sign of feeling punished by the humidity and heat.

Lap 3, Hassan-Kipyegon, running hip to hip. The real wheat.

The bell lap, lap 4, is a decisive moment. Those two hang with each other. But after 200 meters more, Kipyegon shifts the narrative. She pulls away as she runs the curve, her spikes hammering into the track. And as she sprints, the gap between herself and Hassan widens. It's as though Kipyegon is being magnetically pulled forward. Her stride is wide and rhythmic. She is closing in on another part of her dream. Close becomes closer. And closer and closer down the homestretch. She pumps her left fist in the air just seconds before her feet stamp across lane one in 3:53:11.

How symbolic.

And just like that, the mother, who is an athlete, is also an Olympic champion—and a new Olympic record holder. Kipyegon's time reset a standard that had stood for 33 years, and she became the first woman to win back-to-back Olympic gold since the Soviet Union's Tatyana Kazankina did so in two consecutive Olympics.

Muir comes through a second later, silver, followed by Hassan another second later, bronze.

Kipyegon kneels down and plants her face on the ground, simultaneously slapping her hands on the track. Five years ago in Rio, the fate was similar, but different. She had won, but there was no daughter to think about as she crossed the finish line a winner, unlike in this moment, when her child is among her first thoughts.

Kipyegon lifts herself from the ground, shaking her head no. But *yes*, this is real. This is all very real. She kisses her fingers and waves to the mostly empty stadium.

A glorious moment.

A quiet, glorious moment.

A quiet, glorious moment that became a highlight of her career.

A quiet, glorious moment that became a highlight of Sang's year.

Proud is his immediate thought, one he texts moments after Kipyegon catches a Kenyan flag tossed from the sideline.

So many early mornings of her feet stepping onto the floor in the dark, awake before sunrise to prepare for another bout of working toward this quiet, glorious moment. So many days living at camp in Kaptagat, away from her husband and daughter. A necessary sacrifice for this quiet, glorious moment. So many times the high altitude stole her breath as she nourished her mind to handle this quiet, glorious moment. So many occasions Sang shouted "Hey, Superstar!"—chuckling yet sincere about his nickname for Kipyegon.

"In the olden days, whenever a lady would get married, sports would go out the window," Sang says. To have a husband and one's family rallying behind her, believing in her and letting her live at training camp six days a week to be handled by other people—as in the coaching staff and management and being around her campmates more than her family—"that takes a lot of understanding."

"When you have a child and you're a mother, there are expectations. The child has expectations, the husband, the community. I give a lot of credit to Faith. You have to have your own diplomatic way of managing the nucleus," Sang continues.

Kipyegon, he says, proves that women are limitless.

She wraps the Kenyan flag around her body like a cape, her face beaming as she hoists her arms above her head.

Thousands of miles away, her daughter is watching. And on screens all over the world women are watching.

This is her *Why*.

THE OTHER SIDE OF THE LINE

Sang's silver medal from the 1992 Barcelona Olympics is in his house. Somewhere. "I think it's in a safe," he says. He doesn't have a medal from his first Olympics—1988 Seoul, South Korea. That Olympics had included Soviet athletes. The Soviet Union had not yet dissolved. The Cold War had not yet ended. It was an Olympics described as both exciting and ripe with tension.

Not all National Olympic Committees participated in the Seoul Games (the Democratic People's Republic of Korea {North Korea} along with Cuba, Ethiopia, and Nicaragua withdrew). "Those were the things I was looking at more than individual achievement," Sang recalls. "The whole situation was overwhelming." They were to be the largest Olympics to date. It was reported in the media that the Olympics cost the South Korean government approximately $3.1 billion, which included a cleanup of the Han River. It was an opportunity for the city, the fifth most populous in the world at the time, to show off. Track and field was described as being among the glamorous sports of the Games, along with basketball, gymnastics, and swimming.

It was predicted that the Soviet Union, the United States, and East Germany would come out on top as lead medal earners. This was the era of American sprinting sensations like Florence Griffith Joyner, the 100- and 200-meter world record holder; Jackie Joyner-Kersee, considered the greatest heptathlete in history; and Carl Lewis, one of the most decorated sprinters and athletes of all time (he would amass nine Olympic gold medals by the end of his career). Indeed, track and field was a sport to pay close attention to.

The opening ceremony began on September 17 at the Olympic Stadium, nine days before the start of the men's steeplechase, which was organized into three qualifying heats, two semi-finals, and the final. Of the 33 competitors among the entry list,* 26 would make the cut into the semi-finals. The number would shrink to 13 for the final on September 30, a Friday.

Sang was there with fellow Kenyan Julius Kariuki, who had one Olympic experience under his feet. Kariuki competed four years prior at the Los Angeles Olympics and placed seventh. Peter Koech was also in the mix. He was not yet the world record holder in the event. That would come a year later, in 1989. This was the offering Kenya had sent to uphold the country's reputation in the event. Steeplechase was becoming increasingly dominated by Kenya at the Olympics, won first in 1968 by Amos Biwott, followed by Kip Keino in 1972, then Julius Korir in 1984 in Los Angeles.

The whole experience of suiting up in Kenya's national colors was Sang's driving force. What he remembers from these Olympic Games is mostly that he was happy to be there. "Really, that's the bottom line. I was happy to have represented my country," Sang says. "The whole atmosphere was fantastic. The Koreans went out of their way to make people happy."

Sang started his Olympic experience in the third round of qualifying heats. He won and advanced to the semi-final, where he competed in the first heat and placed fourth. The top three times of each semi-final advanced to the final. Sang lined up among 12 other men.

---

* 33 athletes were on the starting list (30 athletes ranked, 1 disqualified, 2 did not start).

ABOVE: Patrick Sang (third row, third from right) with the University of Texas track team. In 1982, Sang accepted a scholarship offer after assistant track and field coach James Blackwood had visited Kenya for a recruiting trip. *Courtesy of Texas Athletics.* BELOW: As an undergraduate at the University of Texas, Patrick Sang was a member of the track and field and cross country programs from 1983 until he graduated in 1986 with a bachelor's degree in economics and a minor in geography. *Courtesy of Texas Athletics.*

Patrick Sang won the conference title in the steeplechase three times, and he still holds the University of Texas school record (8:22.45) for the event. *Courtesy of Texas Athletics.*

Patrick Sang owns 5 of the top-10 times ever run in the steeplechase for the University of Texas. *Courtesy of Texas Athletics.*

James Blackwood, formerly the assistant coach for track and field and cross country at the University of Texas. Blackwood guided Patrick Sang throughout his collegiate athletic career. *Courtesy of Texas Athletics.*

ABOVE: Patrick Sang (left) with countrymen Mathew Birir (center) and William Mutwol (right) after competing in the 3,000-meter steeplechase at the 1992 Barcelona Olympics. Sang, who won a silver medal, helped Kenya sweep the podium in the event for the first time in history. *Courtesy of Bob Martin/Allsport.* BELOW: Members of Global Sports Communication training camp prepare for a run before sunrise. *Courtesy of NN Running Team.*

ABOVE: Long runs upwards of 40K in Kaptagat, Kenya, are often accompanied by a support car. Patrick Sang and his coaching staff follow the elites and hand out fluid bottles at roughly 5 kilometer increments. *Courtesy of Jason Suarez.* BELOW: Athletes around Kaptagat often join members of Global Sports Communication training camp for training sessions. Patrick Sang estimates around 80 percent of the runners in an average session he is voluntarily coaching. *Courtesy of Jason Suarez.*

ABOVE: A morning long run through Kaptagat Forest in Kenya, which is part of a training loop that runners refer to as "The Boston Route", appropriately named due to stretches of long, rolling hills. The route reaches approximately 2,700 meters (8,858 feet) above sea level. *Courtesy of Sarah Gearhart.* BELOW: Hearing impaired athlete David Kipkogei (center) during a long run in Kaptagat, Kenya. Though he is not a member of Global Sports Communication training camp, he has been showing up to train with Patrick Sang's group since 2019. *Courtesy of Sarah Gearhart.*

Marathon world record holder Eliud Kipchoge (second from right) with Global Sports Communication training camp partners, who are also members of the NN Running Team, the first professional running team in the world, founded by Jos Hermens in 2017. The NN Running Team comprises more than 60 elite runners worldwide. *Courtesy of NN Running Team.*

ABOVE: Patrick Sang in Kaptagat, Kenya. *Courtesy of NN Running Team.* BELOW: Patrick Sang during a training session with assistant coach Richard Metto. *Courtesy of NN Running Team.*

ABOVE: A speed training session takes place on the dirt track at Global Sports Communication training camp in Kaptagat, Kenya. The track, which extends 380 meters, 20 shy of a standard version, was constructed in 2020 during the coronavirus pandemic. *Courtesy of Sarah Gearhart.* BELOW: Patrick Sang with athletes at Global Sports Communication training camp in Kaptagat, Kenya. *Courtesy of NN Running Team.*

ABOVE: Faith Kipyegon won gold in the women's 1,500 meters at the 2020 Tokyo Olympics, her third consecutive Games. She set a new 1,500-meter record and became only the second woman in history to win back-to-back Olympic titles in the event. *Copyright © Getty Images.* BELOW: Geoffrey Kamworor runs through the winners tape during the 2019 New York City Marathon. It was his second victory at the largest major marathon in the world. With more than 50,000 finishers annually, the race attracts one of the most competitive elite fields in the sport. *Copyright © Getty Images.*

Geoffrey Kamworor embraces training partner, mentor and friend Eliud Kipchoge after winning his first New York City Marathon title in 2017. *Copyright © Getty Images.*

ABOVE: The "raw talent" as Patrick Sang describes of the Athletics Kenya Central Rift Under-20 pre-trials, which skims a handful of the best amateur runners that move on to a national meet. *Courtesy of Sarah Gearhart.* BELOW: Global Sports Communication training camp junior athlete Jackline Chepkoech (center) approaches the starting line for the steeplechase at the Athletics Kenya Central Rift Under-20 pre-trials. She won and later advanced to the World Athletics U20 Championship, where she was crowned a champion. *Courtesy of Sarah Gearhart.*

ABOVE: Global Sports Communication performance director Valentijn Trouw (left), Patrick Sang (center) and Global Sports Communication founder and CEO Jos Hermens (right) at the 2019 New York City Marathon. *Courtesy of NN Running Team.* BELOW: Patrick Sang on the field during a track session. *Courtesy of NN Running Team.*

Patrick Sang with youth runners at the Discovery Kenya Cross Country Championships in Eldoret in January 2022. The event is one of the most important youth races in the country. *Courtesy of Sarah Gearhart.*

Portrait of Patrick Sang. *Courtesy of Pim Rinkes.*

Patrick Sang embraces Eliud Kipchoge after his 2:01:39 world record performance at the 2018 Berlin Marathon. Kipchoge would smash the world record again in 2022 with a time of 2:01:09 in Berlin. *Courtesy of Jason Suarez.*

When the race went off, he attempted to make a move with three laps remaining alongside Italian Alessandro Lambruschini. Sang's teammates Kariuki and Koech took off with two laps to go and ran mostly unchallenged. Kariuki ultimately broke away and ran to an Olympic record. Koech was one second behind. The duo would stand 1-2 on the podium. Sang finished seventh overall. Admittedly, earning a medal wasn't his goal at the time. "I should have thought about going further," he reflects 33 years later. "Of course, it was not possible. The competition was too advanced. The times were fast." He adds, "I came out with zero regrets."

His objective would change after the Olympic Games in South Korea. Four years later, going into the Barcelona Olympics, Sang had a different agenda. This time around, in Spain, he wanted a place on the podium. "I'd grown in a way that I really understood what was at stake. I realized that is what's valued. That's what makes the sport spin. That's what makes the sponsors pay attention," Sang says.

His leadership position as team captain would influence his coaching method in the future at Global Sports Communication training camp. Being in a leadership role is a lesson for oneself. You engage your brain more when you are in charge of other people, he says.

At camp, he likes to put individuals who are "nowhere close to the top athletes," as he puts it, in leadership positions as a way for that individual to grow. "Interestingly, these people who have been appointed to leadership positions, they've used that opportunity to push themselves to another level."

———

Sang and his support staff, which includes assistant coach Richard Metto and physiotherapist Peter Nduhui, arrive in Japan just a few days before competitions end on August 8. Sapporo versus Tokyo. Tokyo versus Sapporo. Sang can't be in two places at once, so he is on location 500 miles north of the capital for the men's and women's marathon. When he arrives in Sapporo and throughout his visit, he doesn't interact much with anybody. Not that there's opportunity.

The experience at these Olympics Games is . . . different. Compared to five years ago at the Rio Olympics and other previous Olympics he attended as a coach, like in Beijing in 2008, when China engaged in weather engineering in the form of cloud seeding to keep away rain and also to lower the high levels of pollution, he remembers.

At the 1992 Games in Barcelona, at least international spectators could show up to watch the action unfold in person, like what Sang's college coach James Blackwood did. As Sang was running a victory lap after Kenya had swept the podium, he heard Blackwood shouting his name.

Blackwood had contacted Sang in advance to let him know that he would be in the stands. "I was down at the end," Blackwood recalls after Birir, Sang, and Mutwol finished 1, 2 and 3. "They all came over to where I was. People standing around thought I'd coached all three," he says, laughing. "My wife had a camera. She started crying. She missed the picture of me and the three Kenyans!"

After Sang received his medal, he returned to the stands and sat with his college coach "for a long, long time," Blackwood remembers. "We had to move to the end [of the seats] because people were coming up for his autograph. I thought that was kind of cool."

Blackwood thought Sang had a chance to win the steeplechase. "He was very cautious going over that last barrier," he remembers watching. "Later he told me he was very concerned [during the Olympic race] because at the NCAAs one year, he fell in the water jump. He was second the year before. We scored 14 points in the steeple. We lost the NCAA championship by two points. He was thinking about that [while he was in the Olympic race] . . . I think that may have cost him the race. I don't know. It's hard to say what would've happened."

Still, Sang says of his experience in Barcelona, "It was a proud moment for me and also for the guy who gave me a chance to go that route."

In contrast now, Sang is on the other side of the line in support of the athletes he gave a chance to go this route.

"When my athletes are competing, that feeling comes back," he says, referring to the adrenaline, the excitement. As a coach, "there's a unique tension when you get to a competition. You feel stressed in a special way. But it's a positive stress. It's part of the game."

The tension is particularly unique as these Games. In Sapporo, police are lined up around the perimeter of the hotel. And everywhere. According to one European Olympic marathoner, one cannot branch out, or else they are quickly tended to by guards.

Athletes are not allowed into the nearby Makomanai Park to train during the days leading up to the Olympic marathon. Instead, they are limited to running in Makomanai Stadium and a 900-meter loop around its perimeter.

"I don't want to blame the Japanese. It's something [the Olympics] that should not have happened. It was forced on them," Sang says.

The infection rate shoots up during the Games, even despite efforts to suppress spectators, who have a vicarious experience through televised programming at odd hours due to the drastic difference in time zones. Japan is 14 hours ahead of the eastern part of the US, 17 hours ahead of the West Coast, 8 hours ahead of much of Europe, and 6 hours ahead of East Africa.

On Sunday morning, August 8, 2021, "we are going to witness history," one commentator said pre-race. "Eliud Kipchoge is going to do the one thing left on his CV."

That one thing left is to defend the men's marathon title. If Kipchoge is successful, he will become the third man in history to accomplish the remarkable feat. His name would be mentioned alongside Ethiopian Abebe Bikila (1960, 1964) and Waldemar Cierpinski of East Germany (1976, 1980).

The weight of favoritism: either fold or ride the wave.

"Treat yourself as the best one," Sang had told Kipchoge during a training session back in 2003. "I still remember, it's fresh in my mind," Kipchoge says.

"From that day I was really treating myself as the best one in training and in racing. When you're standing on the line, you want to compete. You should actually tell your mind you are competing with high-profile marathoners, but I am the best-trained person. There is no way that they can beat me. That's how to treat yourself as the best," Kipchoge says.

Kipchoge will have to beat 105 other men—including fellow countrymen Amos Kipruto and Lawrence Cherono—to win. And he must do so in inhospitable conditions. *Searing* would be a more honest word.

On race day, the sun is beaming in Sapporo, and the temperature warms to 78.8 degrees Fahrenheit with 80 percent humidity already by 7 A.M. Before they'd even step to the starting line, athletes can be seen walking around with ice vests. The conditions are concerning. Humidity can drastically affect the body's ability to cool itself. When the humidity is high, moisture can stay on the skin longer, resulting in feeling even hotter. Despite the aggravating weather, the athletes must accept the situation. No one wants a DNF label, as in did not finish. So they are each prepared to roll the dice.

Fortunately, this marathon course is pancake flat. It begins in Odori Park and traces the heart of the city. At least part of the route is shaded, a necessary detail when running in the heat for 26.2 miles.

A marathon is already a fight with the body. Internally and externally, the journey can be unpredictable. Like a chess match, cerebral, but much, much more physical. The saying is, when racing, the moment the mind goes, the body goes. The mind and body must be connected, Sang has reiterated multiple times. One can be the most seasoned runner and not win.

The main man, Kipchoge, donning bib 2776 on the back of his jersey, "KIPCHOGE" on the front, is ready to chase, following in the footsteps of other countrymen before him who attempted the same grind. Samuel Wanjiru had set the Olympic record in the men's marathon in 2008 in Beijing. Wanjiru is the only other Kenyan man who has won gold in the event at the Olympics. Kipchoge is the second in his country's history.

At the start of the race, Kipchoge is sandwiched between men in white caps, shading their heads from the fiery sun, ready to test whether he can repeat his effort from five years ago in Rio.

What is it really like to line up next to this world record holder and Olympic champion? He's like them: present for a common goal, to race. But unlike them, he is the one the world anticipates will win. Who will attempt to intercept?

The men take off from the line, plugging the street in a mad rush. After more than a decade of a world-leading career across multiple disciplines, Kipchoge is still the man up front. There are no pacers in the Olympic marathon to help usher him and other contenders to the finish. Unlike other races, this one isn't necessarily about achieving a fast time. What matters is earning a place on the podium. This race is about winning. Case in point: when Kipchoge won the marathon at the 2016 Rio Olympics, his 2:08:44 finish was the slowest performance of his marathon career.

Colombian Jeison Alexander Suarez, a guy who runs just inside 2:11, sets the tone early by leading the pack and looking bent on controlling the race. Kipchoge grabs a bottle of water from an aid station and pours it down his neck, quickly bathing his skin in coolness. The heat feels cruel on the body. Aid stations are particularly crucial.

Kipchoge ticked off early kilometers, reaching the 5K mark with more than 20 men in the lead pack. The temperature climbs a degree. The men's and women's marathons were moved north of Tokyo for the welfare of the athletes, but Sapporo is experiencing a heat wave. Still, despite the stifling temperatures, the sidelines are laced with spectators, a detail that would be phrohibited in Tokyo.

Less than 30 minutes into the race, a slew of high-profile contenders begin to unravel in the 79-degree heat. The former Olympic marathon champion Stephen Kiprotich of Uganda, whom Sang also coached to the top of the podium in the past, stops and walks. Ethiopian Shura Kitata clenches his right hamstring on the side of the course as he pauses and eventually pulls out. Tanzanian record holder Gabriel Geay drops from the lead pack.

"We are going to see a major casualty list in this race," a commentator says.

When the temperature ticks up, some athletes do something totally abnormal: stop themselves, attempt to regain composure, and then continue running. Whatever it takes to remain in the game, to retain some form of honor that brought them into this situation—a once-in-a-lifetime opportunity for most of the participants.

Thirty-five minutes into the event, another Ethiopian, Alemu Bekele, stops on the side of the course, before deciding to jog back into the race. The struggles continue for a lot of competitors in the field.

"That's a jog, that's not a run at all," a commentator assesses Kiprotich, who once again pulled off to the side for a moment. Forget about getting onto the podium. These men are trying to hang on.

The struggle doesn't find Kipchoge at the moment. He is in a familiar position, up front, running with no wasted movement. The lead pack begins to disintegrate only around the 15 kilometer mark. There's a point when he fist-bumps a runner from Brazil, Daniel do Nascimento.

Halfway into the race, Kipchoge's name is planted second on the leaderboard, just 0.02 seconds behind number 1. A nominal detail. He still appears relaxed. And he is, considering the projected time of 2:10.

By the 1:20 mark, Kipchoge misses his drink station. Whether or not he's concerned, Kipchoge doesn't wear any emotion on his face.

Just a couple of minutes earlier, he took the reins. He keeps going, "injecting the pace," describes a commentator.

American Galen Rupp, the Olympic bronze medalist from Rio, hangs in the lead pack. Here is Kipchoge, a guy who hasn't flirted with living another lifestyle though he can certainly afford to. Here is a guy who stays attached to his roots. The humble leader, up front. The real wheat. What-you-see-is-what-you-get quality.

When the pack reaches 30 kilometers, there's an obvious chance of a negative split, meaning to run the second half of the race faster than the first.

At 1:43 into the race, Kipchoge makes a move. Those watching see history in the making. He pulls away from the pack and runs on his own. The camera pans to a close-up of him. A slight smile spreads on his face.

With 10 kilometers to the finish, his lead builds to five seconds. The two Kenyans fall to the back of the lead group. The game has shifted from staying with Kipchoge to catching him *if you can*. But likely they can't. The battle instead is for silver and bronze.

Within three kilometers, Kipchoge puts himself 70 meters ahead of the group labeled "Chase 1," four men who will be reduced to two for the other podium spots. Somali-born Abdi Nageeye, representing the Netherlands, and Cherono, one of Kipchoge's teammates, are among them.

A succession of clapping ensues as Kipchoge darts past spectators spilling over the barriers lining the course. His lead grows to 100 meters. His pace quickens. The 5K split reads 14:28. *14:28.* With seven kilometers remaining. Such a time is a life goal for that distance for many runners. To do it at the end of a marathon is nothing short of incredibly impressive.

Kipchoge's lead grows to 1 minute and 30 seconds. There he is, running alone. He grabs a water bottle from the side and pours it down his neck. He looks like he could keep going by the time he reaches 42 kilometers.

Just 195 meters remain. He begins to wave to both sides of the crowd, gives them thumbs-up, too. He smiles as he runs through the finish line tape. A group of photographers feverishly click their cameras.

Kipchoge waits at the finish as Nageeye comes through in second, followed by Bashir Abdi, the Somali-born Belgian. Both had overtaken Kipchoge's teammate, Cherono, on the way. Out of a field of 106 total entrants, 30 had dropped out during the race.

The distance that Kipchoge said yes to years ago has continued to be favorable to him. "It has taught me to restrain," he says. "To persevere."

Equally as much, the marathon has taught him "to really think big," he says.

Kipchoge's win was another highlight of Sang's 2021. "It's amazing when you see somebody believing in what they do and they do it so well," Sang says of Kipchoge. "It's a learning curve for yourself also. It's good to believe in something."

Sang uses the word *stressful* when describing what it felt watching Kipchoge race. But Sang was also proud, a word he doesn't use, but it is obvious in the tone of his voice.

PERPETUAL MOTION

What is it about him that gets the best out of all of you?" Kenyan journalist Jeff Koinange posed the question on TV to Sang's champions, Kipyegon and Kipchoge, after their gold medal performances at the Tokyo Olympics.

Kipchoge quietly considers the question about Sang for a moment. "What's actually the difference between Patrick and other coaches . . ." he begins. "The difference is how to manage the talent, how to expose the talent, and how to identify the talent. And above all, how to make that athlete a human being. In our camp, we want to be the best athletes. At the same time, we want to be human beings."

Social coach. Life coach. Sports coach. "To get a person of that caliber is really hard," Kipchoge says.

The return home has been busy for the Running Royals—as Kipyegon and Kipchoge are referred to—but also for Sang. The clock keeps ticking. Sang is back at camp, resuming business as usual. The fall racing season is underway, which includes one of the sport's most popular events, the Berlin Marathon. "I will never get tired of Berlin," Sang has said. Apart from the high-level organization and phenomenal support all around, the course has special significance. Kipchoge broke the marathon world record in the German capital in 2018. Sang's athletes are no strangers to the course as well.

A part of Kenya is being shown here at the 2021 edition of the Berlin Marathon. While Kipchoge is absent due to having just successfully defended his Olympic title, his training partner Josphat Boit is on site.

Race preparations are visible 10 days out from the Berlin Marathon. Signage stamped around various parts of the course advise where not to park on this sacred Sunday, September 26. After a year hiatus due to the pandemic, roughly 35,000 runners will stampede through the city.

Berlin is considered the fastest major marathon course in the world, and there's an elevated suspense as to who will trace it first. That is, who will attempt to chase Kipchoge's 2:01:39 world record, set on this ground with Boit by his side as the final pacemaker in 2018.

The path starts at 38 meters above sea level and peaks at 53 meters, paling in comparison to the 2,400 meters that guys like Boit are used to in Kaptagat. Boit will contend with a dozen other prospects, who include Ethiopian Kenenisa Bekele, the fastest entrant in the field, whose 2019 Berlin mark is only seconds shy of Kipchoge's world record.

Facts like that don't deter Boit. The Kenyan had paced Kipchoge for 25 of 42.1 kilometers in 2018. Then 23, Boit was merely a footnote next to the humble headliner. Boit had agreed to participate in the Berlin Marathon as a pacer after having clocked 59:19 at the Lago Maggiore Half Marathon in Italy in April 2018. He references that season as his peak year. Having joined Global Sports Communication training camp just months prior only escalated his athletic progress.

Sometimes Boit can't believe he's living his dream—that he is privileged to be attached to the same camp he'd known as being for "big names only."

"You know it is rare for someone from nowhere to join some bigger camp. I didn't even believe I had joined," Boit says. Back in 2015, when he was employed by the police force, he'd wondered if he even stood a chance. He wasn't much of a serious runner, he says. Not yet.

As an officer in training during 2015, Boit would join the police force's athletics team. He quickly adjusted to morning runs upward of 30 kilometers and twice-weekly speed sessions. It was a small taste of life as a professional runner. Reality would shift in 2017, when he competed in 5,000 meters at the National Police Service Athletics Championship in Nairobi. The effect of winning the event was that his coach at the time encouraged Boit to try to join Global Sports Communication training camp.

Prior to being received by the camp, Boit had already known that Sang had produced many successful athletes over the years: steeplechase Olympic champions Reuben Kosgei and Brimin Kipruto; 5,000 meter world champion Richard Limo; as well as Felix Limo, who has won three major marathons (Berlin, Chicago, and London). The list runs deep. As an insider, though, it clicked with Boit how much of an opportunity it really is to be guided by Sang.

"Coach Sang is a very silent person," Boit says. "Sometimes, if he wants to tell you something, he cannot tell you directly. He will say something, and you will go and digest it."

This is a man, Boit says, who wants to keep the mind active. Think fast. "I think he's trying to make you ready for everything. Ready for life."

"Coach likes for someone to be independent. There are some other coaches that follow you here and there. He says, 'You know what brought you here. And you know what you are doing here. When you are grown up like this, I will not follow you. You do what you're supposed to do.'"

Three years ago, though, Sang was here in Berlin. The morning of September 16, 2018, was primed for something special. A pale blue sky dotted with creamy pillowy puffs; 57 degrees Fahrenheit—not too hot, not too cool. A perfect day to slip on a pair of running shoes and run a marathon.

No one—not race director Mark Milde, not even a handful of the world's top distance runners, and especially not the 1 million spectators lining the course in Berlin—knew how the next 2 hours, 1 minute, and

39 seconds were about to unfold. Not even the man who was poised to do it. But Sang knew.

He just knew.

Former champion Kenyan Dennis Kimetto, who set a course record in 2014, describes the Berlin Marathon as "the best in the world." Year after year, the race attracts some of the top distance runners globally.

And on this occasion, Kipchoge showed up for his fourth Berlin Marathon appearance. A handful of pacemakers surrounded him the moment the starting gun snapped. Sang watched as Kipchoge began to make his way through the city.

Not much had been adjusted in Kipchoge's training plan leading into this race. A little extra physiotherapy and more strength training was about all that Sang had added. He admitted that he felt comfortable with Kipchoge's work prior to the race and was convinced he was prepared to chase—not anyone else but himself, the man designated with bib number 1 pinned on the back of his white tank top.

Kipchoge rolled through the first 10 kilometers in 29:21. By the 15 kilometer mark, two of the three pacers dropped out. Around mile 15, the last pacer, Boit, let go, leaving Kipchoge to endure the remaining 10 and a half miles alone.

Three hundred meters from the famous Brandenburg Gate—the iconic landmark symbolizing unity and freedom after the fall of the Berlin Wall—the race was Kipchoge's. A BMW lead pace car trailed behind with a digital clock ticking on top.

"He must have dreamed of these moments. He must have gone through these sights in his mind," one sportscaster said.

The clock ticked to 2:01:05. Fifty meters remained. The crowd continued to erupt. "Music to my ears," Kipchoge later admitted. A smile spread across his face. Perhaps he smiles because the world record is about to be his.

And it was, after 2 hours, 1 minute, and 39 seconds. More than a minute faster than the previous world record (2:02:57). "Grateful,"

Kipchoge later said of his achievement. Prior to this moment, he admitted he had merely wanted to run a personal best. It was described as the greatest performance in the history of the marathon.

Kipchoge patted his head with both hands after he crossed the finish line with a wide-open smile. Elation. He ran into the arms of Sang, who lifted Kipchoge off the ground as they hugged tightly.

Sang shivered. He shivered at the thought when Kipchoge came to see him as a teen. He says that it never occurred to him, until Kipchoge set this world record in Berlin, that he could have easily turned the young runner away that day in Nandi County, when he eagerly prodded Sang.

"Suppose I had told him, 'Get lost,'" Sang muses. "Whether it was fate or not, the fact that I [didn't] chase him away . . . Suppose I had said no?"

PUSHING

He can quit anytime.

When his muscles tighten, leaving his body uncomfortably numb.

When his lungs plead for more air.

When cramps pinch with arresting tension.

He can quit anytime.

When a blister balloons on his feet, the friction a piercing pain.

When his body boxes with his mind.

He can quit anytime.

When his competitor pulls ahead, the speed unmatched.

When the finish line seems to stretch.

When the last mile is more punishing than the others.

He can quit anytime.

When his legs begin to lose the fight.

When his goal slips out of sight.

He can quit anytime.

But he keeps going.

Inside room 311 at the WestCord Fashion Hotel in Amsterdam, Laban Korir lay in bed, eyes closed as he prays. A thought permeates his mind. He is thinking about a number. *Let me be among the top guys.*

Immeasurable hours and weeks of preparation for the Amsterdam Marathon will define him as a statistic in the world of sports. But in the world outside of sports, Korir is a man attached to values learned by running toward that number. *Who are you beyond an athlete?* is a question he's been indirectly coached by Sang to ruminate.

Saturday, October 16, 2021, the day before the race, Korir quietly waits for an early wake-up call to retrace his footsteps. He speaks softly about memories of his racing experiences on this course, like finishing second in 2011, and achieving his personal best for the marathon in 2016 (2:05:54). Exterior results from an interior pursuit. For his effort on this occasion, Korir wants to dig into 2:04.

Korir arrived two days prior by way of 10 hours suspended in the air—Eldoret to Nairobi to Paris to Amsterdam. Journeying from Kaptagat's high altitude to below sea level in the Netherlands' capital is like offering his lungs a break—until the moment he lines up alongside his training partners, Jonathan Korir and Eritrean Merhawi Kesete, who are also here to prove something too.

Pre-race, Sang had texted his athletes: "Run smart." Whatever that means is for each athlete to determine on his own. "When he tells you something, you have to think," Korir says of Sang. "What is the meaning? Sometimes it's difficult to understand."

"That's who I am," Sang says. He speaks in a conversation of parables. "You see, when you speak in parables, you force people to listen. A parable has a deeper meaning. I can talk to an athlete in front of 100 people and the other guys will hear whatever I'm saying has a story. But the message will only go to the right person."

"He makes me think"—even Kipchoge will admit. One can learn about Sang's mind simply by having a conversation with his athletes. "They can also tell you I'm a very difficult person," Sang says, laughing.

It took time for Korir to catch on—and catch up. He knew of Sang before he joined Global Sports Communication training camp more than a decade ago. Korir was a regular at training sessions, though he lived on his own outside the camp. Silent and serious was his immediate impression of Sang. "I was so afraid of him," says Korir, who questioned whether he belonged with the elite of the elite. "A small junior joining a big team," he remembers. "I was very shy." It's taken a while for Korir to grow into himself and believe he has a place, earned only after a labyrinth of struggles.

When Korir talks about his upbringing, down and poor, in his words, he speaks about the tragedy of his father dying when he was a young boy. Korir's mother sold the family's land in Nandi Hills and moved to Koisagat village in Lessos "to meet other ladies that could assist," as he says of his mother's motive. She'd tote herself around to other villages and ask to borrow money so she could pay the fees to keep her kids in school and go somewhere else in life. Sometimes her hustling was enough. Other times, Korir and his siblings shared in her struggle. When money was drained, as it often was, education became a rotating opportunity. Korir repeatedly sacrificed his schooling, staying at home for extended periods, affording his siblings to go instead.

When Korir was 17, he took a job at a small restaurant making chapati, chai, and African donuts known as mandazi. He worked from morning until as late as 8 P.M., earning roughly 50 shillings (50 cents) a day. The monthly income of 1,500 shillings ($15) helped put meals on the table.

When his hands weren't rolling out and frying dough, he'd run off to train with friends, at the encouragement of a teacher who had asked Korir to consider competing. No matter his limited resources, he followed wherever running took him, like to Kipchoge Keino Stadium in Eldoret to participate in a 10,000-meter race at a district meet. Korir's feet were black after he finished barefoot in fourth place.

His work, work, run, work, work, run rhythm only slightly altered after he had carefully saved slivers of his monthly 1,500 shillings for three years. In 2005, Korir had just enough to afford a small cow and a Yashica camera (for the equivalent of $70 combined), the latter of which he bought from a friend, who taught him how to use the camera. He traded making mandazis for walking around his village from one house to another and taking portraits, charging 30 shillings (30 cents) per photo. It was more opportune during holidays, like Christmas. Sometimes Korir was hired to take photos at weddings. His business was stable enough to consistently help support the family.

Life as a photographer ceased when he moved to Kaptagat to develop his running career at the suggestion of a friend he knew from his primary school days. "He told me to go and stay in his room outside of the camp. I was expecting everything to be there," Korir says. But there was nothing, not even a small bag of maize flour to cook a few meals of ugali.

Going home wasn't an option. He had mentally projected the village gossip. *He can't handle the training. Weak.* Those thoughts alone were all the motivation Korir needed. It's better to work harder than simply work hard, so "I worked and worked," he says.

To cover rent of 1,000 shillings ($10) and buy food, Korir again took a job at a small restaurant, standing on his feet up to 12 hours a day, making chapatis and mandazis and going back and forth to Sang's training sessions six days a week. He never let on about his situation.

No one really knows what those outside of camp who come every morning to train with Sang's group have to do to consistently show up. No one sees the way they hustle to earn just enough to maintain themselves, all so they can wake up and chase their desired future.

"I know there are some who are suffering," Korir says of the current slate of athletes. Walk the path and you know. "You look at the person. You can look in the face. You can see," says training partner Jonathan. You can see *this is someone in need.*

The awareness develops an obligation. Yes, both men say simultaneously, without pause, they're indebted to contribute what they can to reduce another's struggle. "An athlete helped us to reach where we are now," Korir says. Clothes, shoes to train in, money for food and rent. Korir empathizes with that feeling of living with slender resources but with the will to become better. They both say it was Sang who taught them how to pay it forward. That it's a necessary part of life.

Sometimes Sang will pick a few runners from outside camp who have consistently showed up and proved a genuine commitment. "After you finish, come and see Laban," Sang told them a few weeks before Korir flew to Amsterdam. The seniors at camp were asked to share something extra, a T-shirt, a jacket, a pair of shoes, to reward the efforts of the runners less than materially, but equally dedicated.

Korir makes it a priority when he travels to a race to bring back training apparel and running shoes. During this journey to the Amsterdam Marathon, that will include a couple of duffel bags stuffed with new running gear. "If you stay with someone who helps people, like Patrick, you will be like him," he says.

"I have a lot of respect for people who put in the effort," Sang says. "I reward effort. When you reward effort, you are encouraging more people."

There's a guy from outside camp that one of Sang's assistant coaches wanted to chase away. "I told him no. Don't chase this guy. He has not bothered you. He's going to run on a public road, so what is your business?" Sang says. "So the next thing, I got an oversized T-shirt. The guy is big. I went to the village where he stays, and I gave it to him. The guy was so happy. The guy has been consistent. When he's with a crowd, you don't see, but I would see from one and half years back. He was always finishing training consistently. I started motivating him, giving him small things. Recognizing him in front of everybody. This guy works hard."

Those are small things that Sang's college coach Blackwood did for him. When Sang qualified for NCAAs during a meet at UCLA, "the guy cried," he says of Blackwood. He then bought groceries for Sang.

Blackwood, Sang says, taught him fundamental basics of how to live. "That's why I want my athletes to be human beings and not [just] athletes," he says.

"An athlete's life is very short," Sang continues. "If you become a human being in society, you can serve humanity for a long time."

Of course, earning money from a successful performance also affords Korir to expand his reach. But racing for money is not the objective. "When you are preparing for your races, he tells us don't think about money. Don't think about investments." Keep the motivation clear. "First you have to focus on your races, and then these other things will follow. Even Eliud used to tell us that," Korir says.

"We normally have some programs where we bring professionals," Sang says. "The way I got the opportunity to be shaped on financial matters and understand the world of finance was through my interaction with the Swiss. The Swiss system is what we want to expose athletes to so that when they run into money, at least you'll have done something to give them an understanding of handling money." In the past, Sang had also thought about starting an investment club at camp.

Sang says he sees all the time how athletes "hang themselves" before they receive any earnings from a race—they spend what they don't yet have and run into debt.

"Money cannot develop character," Sang says, adding that individuals polish their own character. "When money comes, it's like icing. But the cake has to be there, and that cake has to be made by you."

A life lesson to complement another that Sang talks about: live simply. "I will not change my life. Most of us in the camp are the same," Korir says in reference to the race success among his training partners. "Everybody is equal. That's what he has instilled."

Korir's prayer for his race in Amsterdam will go unanswered.

He had started the marathon according to plan, with the chase group as the race took off just outside of the Olympic Stadium in the Old-South neighborhood. Overcast and 54 degrees Fahrenheit on a famously flat course, the conditions were inviting for a successful performance.

But the thing about racing is one can show up to the starting line as prepared as their counterparts, and yet their master plan can unravel. The marathon can be an unpredictable journey. A side stitch, dehydration, tight quads, hamstring cramps, stomach issues, a blister. Physical derailments. *The pace is too fast. My body is tired. My muscles are burning.* Mental derailments. Running a marathon is an art in conditioning the mind just as much as the body. Where the mind goes, the body follows, as Sang will say.

He knows firsthand the mental and physical bandwidth required in racing, especially at the highest level, and not just for the steeplechase, but in the marathon as well. Sang understands this on this course, too. His footsteps have been here, in October 1999, when he ran the Amsterdam Marathon. It was his second of two marathons he participated in that year; he had run Rotterdam in the spring, his first attempt at the distance, and clocked 2:15.

At the 1999 Amsterdam Marathon, when Kenya swept both the men's and women's titles, Sang's 2:14 performance became his personal best of the few marathons he would run in his career (that included Prague and Amsterdam twice).

"The marathon is taxing. The mental strength of people is something that really needs to be studied," Sang says.

Korir rushed the best he could to finish in 2:07:55, 17th place overall—two pages deep in the online results. The man who wore bib number 7 described the effort as underperforming. "I was expecting that I would be among the guys who are running 2:04," he says.

In the world of the elite of the elite, it is minutes behind the 2021 world-leading mark of 2:02:57, set by Kenyan Titus Ekiru at the Milan Marathon in May. Laban Kipngetich Korir ranked barely in the top 100 in the world, as a result of his 2:07 performance. *Competitive* is an understatement to describe the reality of the men's marathon at the highest stage. What would be a lifetime achievement for someone else is a disappointing day for him. The global average marathon time, by the way, is between 4:20 to 4:30.

Korir retreats back to the hotel, back to his room, back to his bed, where he lies, deadpan. His body will revisit the training process all over after a few weeks of recovery. And he will take it through another cycle of 100-mile weeks, achy muscles, lactic acid fighting with his calves, sweat cascading down his back every day for months. *He can quit anytime.*

But he will keep going.

TRADE-OFF

A baby girl wails, but her mother doesn't know it. Instead, mother is consumed by her own feet softly clapping the ground. Mother is occupied by the goal of becoming a champion.

What's it like to be a Kenyan mother who is a 2:21 marathoner? For 36-year-old Selly Chepyego, it's being too out of range to understand what her 14-month-old daughter Brianna needs.

To be fed?

To be put down for a nap?

To have her diaper changed?

To be held just for a tender moment by the woman who gave her life?

Chepyego's mother is answering to baby Brianna. She is the primary caretaker while six days a week Chepyego lives at the training camp, where she sleeps in a twin-sized bed away from the infant girl who likes to cling to her shoulders like a baby koala. In Chepyego's arms, Brianna is quiet and erupts into smiles. "An easy baby," Chepyego said in May 2021 at her home in Kaptagat, a 10-minute drive from camp.

That was a different life, when Chepyego could wrap her arms around Brianna, play with her in the sunshine, laugh at her laugh, smile at her smile, lay her down to sleep. All the while Chepyego knew a different version of motherhood would exist in a few months' time.

Chepyego forgives the necessary reality of being away. A sacrifice? "It is."

Life in Kenya, as they say. A top marathoner in her prime must see through the need to work away from her child. At least, *this caliber* athlete at *this camp*.

Breastfeeding ceased at nine months, so Chepyego could get back to what's at stake: a potential marathon title in early 2022. While the specific race has yet to be announced publicly, she has her eyes on the Tokyo Marathon, Sunday, March 6. March, approximately four months from today, October 28. Devotion doesn't rest when you're aiming to take your body through 26.2 miles in less than 2 hours and 20 minutes. Devotion doesn't rest when you're aiming to win.

So, watch your baby grow up every day? Or experience her by scrolling through a photo album on your cell phone to catch a glimpse of her sweet smile as you keep working to secure her future so that she can grow up without reliving your childhood struggles?

Brianna is starting to talk. "Mama!" she'll blurt into the phone when Chepyego video calls to check on her, "not every day of the week." Chepyego knows that could cause Brianna to panic. Brianna smiles and kisses the phone screen at the sight of Mama. Who misses who more? "I miss her more. She needs me more." Chepyego's voice is soft and honest.

The truth is that Chepyego needs to be away to funnel her energy and focus. At this camp, one comes "for the discipline, for the mission," she simply puts it. Chepyego moved back to Global Sports Communication training camp in August 2021. She counts on one hand the number of women currently living here. Five. Compared to three dozen men. Chepyego is not alone in her endeavor to be at the top of the sport. But she is trying to do so as a mother. Campmate Kipyegon has repeatedly proved to herself, to other athletes at the training camp, to her young daughter and to women around the world, that motherhood hasn't slowed her down. Though Chepyego participates in a different discipline than Kipyegon (the marathon versus 1,500 meters), having a champion like Kipyegon around is a powerful reminder that she can do it.

Being at camp helps Chepyego cope with the separation, not just from baby Brianna, but also from her other two children, Brian, age 14, and Brilliant, age 4. All three are 70 kilometers away, two hours by car. Naturally, when Chepyego is with them, they want her attention. If she were at home, she imagines life after long runs up to 40K—constantly being pulled away by visitors, feeding, and entertaining them when she should be resting. "Training then becomes useless," she says.

Camp is a haven, the place that gives her "peace of mind" to put in the work. She has lived here on and off since 2006, with a 10-year interlude in Japan. She likes the environment and learning from her mentor, Kipchoge. "I chose him." Just like everyone at camp selects what athlete they want to be mentored by.

"Nothing has changed," she says of Kipchoge, whom she's known since 2003.

When Chepyego was reclaiming her form—and confidence—after maternity, he had told her, "Selly, just compare yourself when you're coming back from an injury. There is no difference. This person is healing mentally from the injury. And now you are healing mentally this way. It's almost the same. It's only the mind that you have to set."

"The mind is everything." A line from Sang, passed on to Kipchoge, passed on to Chepyego, who vocalizes this, too. Her silence when she runs says what words cannot.

At 5:39 A.M., the last Thursday in October, the dark empty roads in Kaptagat aren't caked with mud. Rainy season is on pause, affording more flexibility for training, like a 40K run on dirt paths. Long, lean legs half wrapped in black shorts, feet dressed in one of two options, Nike or Adidas, are primed for the occasion.

"Where've you been?" Sang asks a guy in a blue Adidas jacket. "I see you 30 percent of the time." He laughs at the truth.

Abel Kurui, Victor Chumo, and Emmanuel Mutai (once "a 2:03 guy") are clustered in a group of 14 men to the left of Sang. Fourteen more stand to the right.

"If you don't finish, don't expect to jump in the car," jokes assistant coach Richard Metto, whom Sang also refers to as "The Boss."

Sang pulls Janet Ruguru, who debuted in the marathon four days prior, 2:27 in Paris. He comments that she looked like she thought she'd win, the way she led for part of the race. She didn't listen to the words he tells every athlete pre-race: "Run smart." Still, 2:27. It's good. Very good. Sang plucks Kurui from the crowd and brings him in front of Ruguru.

"Police mwenzangu. Pongezi sana," Kurui says. *My fellow policeman. Congratulations.* Ruguru and Kurui are members of the National Police Service.

He grins and begins to slow clap. Everyone joins the 1-2-3 cadence. Most of these runners relate to the 26.2 mile journey. Even as members of the upper echelon of distance running, who make running a marathon look easy, they all know it's not.

The clapping is a language that translates to "Congratulations on your marathon debut. Congratulations on your top-five finish."

Business moves forward at 6:19 A.M., as feet take off running, all in the same direction, but in three groups.

Chepyego is with her pacer and Jackline Chepkoech, the young steeplechaser with the close-cropped hair who has continued to follow her plan. After Chepkoech had advanced to the World Athletics U20 Championships in August, she went on to win the steeplechase after she raced mostly alone just one lap into the event. Her race was a lifetime best. The emerging talent is out here today to run 20K, half of Chepyego's workout.

Kids dressed in green school uniforms, layered with a sweater to counter the morning chill, walk the same path. Some will journey for 30 minutes, some for up to an hour. A handful of scholarship hopefuls run in the opposite direction of Chepyego. She's too quick for them to see that the woman in their presence is one of the country's Grade A runners. Her 2:21:06 personal best as of October 2021 ranks her 72 among women's top performances of all time.

Chepyego's pacer stays tied to 3:43 per kilometer efforts (roughly 5:59 miles) on repeat. Chepyego could run alone. But without that added benefit of someone push, push, pushing her lungs even more than the 2,400 meter elevation already does. The pacer is from outside the camp. She shows her appreciation in the form of money for his rent with enough left over so he can buy a few kilos of maize flour to make ugali and eat it with a collard green dish called sukuma wiki, Swahili for "push the week." Dinner for seven days.

Six months ago, Chepyego's mind was attached to the hard reality of getting back into "champion shape" after bearing a child. "Shape" versus "champion shape" are different standards. Champion shape is weighing 45 kilos (100 pounds) and being able to repeatedly run 5:30-minute miles (or faster).

Chepyego knows the way. She's had time to learn after her first born, when she leaned on a program she received while living and training in Japan. She also used it after her second born, and then again after her third born. It goes like this: four months postpartum, start walking 10 kilometers a day (roughly six miles). "Walking, just walking." Do that for six weeks. "Every day. Every day." It's preparing the body for movement, she says. Then, after those six weeks, start fartlek training,[*] alternating jogging, then walking then jogging. Do that for 15 to 20 kilometers (nearly a half marathon). But do it "Slowly. Slowly."

After Brianna's birth, Chepyego slept a lot. "I didn't go out. I didn't wash clothes. I didn't do anything. Only eating." A lot. For six months. Porridge made of millet is a staple. The postpartum weight melted off

---

[*]   Fartlek is a Swedish term that translates to "speed play." It is a type of interval training that involves running continuously with short bursts of high intensity sprints.

her body. Not much change in diet. Just a reclaiming of the mind. And training. There is no shortcut back to the top, a tiresome and stressful path, Chepyego admits. She reflects back on the earlier stages. "You are thinking too much, *When will I come back?*"

"You feel a lot of fatigue, both physical and mental." It's part of the process. A sacrifice of sorts? "It is."

There is pain in the quads. They'd shake from lunges, squats, and step aerobics with free weights. Unworked abs were seared by crunches up, up, higher, higher. Another rep when tired. And another rep when soreness wraps even the smallest muscles like ivy. Another. And another.

Where is Chepyego's mind today, when the pacer drops out at 28K, 12 shy of the full workout? His knees. It was only a matter of time before he'd succumb to the pain. He ran with his upper torso slightly slanted to the right, his body compensating. Thick snot sticks to the bottom of his nose. His eyes look nearly charcoal colored in the morning light. Body odor hugs his black shirt. He climbs into a support car, skunking it with the scent of hard work.

Chepyego continues. She retrieves fluid from her 17-ounce Maurten bottle handed from a window of a support car. Not all is consumed, and she's running just 1.4 miles shy of a marathon. Her face is expressionless for the remaining seven and a half miles. Whether she's annoyed or disappointed, perhaps both, perhaps neither, her feet keep striking the ground in an elegant rhythm. Back in the day when she started running, she had no shoes. But that didn't hinder her ability to triumph. Barefoot winning is a type of determination among youth in this part of the country.

It's like Kipchoge's mantra (an international catchphrase): "No human is limited."

Chepyego regurgitates the message. "It's not limited to one's athletic career. It encompasses everyone, everywhere. Everything that you do in your life. Go for it. Even if you are at the bottom, you can find your way back to the top."

kichwa juu

keep your head up

2021 NEW YORK CITY MARATHON

Sang's first trip to New York City was back in 1984. He remembers visiting Harlem and the World Trade Center. The towering skyscrapers. The energy of the city. He remembers a New York of another era. That New York was more affordable than the city today, but was also coupled with the emergence of crack cocaine and crime-ridden streets. Yet it was still a vibrant metropolis, just as it is now, one of the great cities of the world.

Now, the city has cleaned up its act. The streets are safer. New York is still thriving with a breadth of offerings, from business to artistic disciplines and sports. The city annually hosts the largest marathon in the world on the first Sunday in November. More than 50,000 people participate, often entering through a lottery system or fundraising for a charity, the latter of which guarantees entry. But a certain caliber of runner is invited to race.

This is the New York that Kamworor knows.

Kamworor and Sang have experienced this New York together. In 2019, Sang and Kamworor flew to the US for the New York City Marathon—a 15-hour direct flight from Nairobi to JFK airport. Kamworor offered Coach his seat in business class in exchange for Sang's economy version. "These are the fruits of your labor. It has nothing to do with me," Sang told him. "Whoever decided that you go business class had a valuation of what you contribute towards the event."

"These are the things I want the athletes to understand," Sang says later.

Once precious cargo that warranted the upgrade to business class, Kamworor is removed from that treatment at the moment. Sunday afternoon, November 7, 2021. He is at home in Eldoret. His chocolate-colored eyes absorb the image of fellow countryman Albert Korir running inside Central Park. Kamworor's TV is reducing his participation in the 50th New York City Marathon to a vicarious experience. He wanted to run the marathon today. Or rather, win it.

Instead, Kamworor is living eight hours ahead of his 27-year-old countryman and the relatively stacked field that includes race favorite Ethiopian Kenenisa Bekele. After a year hiatus, the streets are plugged in Staten Island, Brooklyn, Manhattan, Harlem, and the Bronx with fans to support one of the world's most celebrated sporting events.

The skyline. The taxis. The steam from manhole covers. The leaves. The bridges. The people. Kamworor's smile widens when he thinks about these details, exotic compared to his world in Kenya. Cattle. Sheep. Maize fields. Iron-colored dirt roads.

"I know New York as a beautiful city," he says. "Unique energy."

It's as though his voice smiles when he replays in his mind running the last 500 meters in Central Park in 2019. "A beautiful decoration of the world flags along the course, the crowd cheering, it motivates," he says.

In 2019 in New York, Kamworor and Korir were on the starting line together, but they finished 23 seconds apart. It was Kamworor's race to own. He sprinted to the end in such a way that it looked as though he was "closing out a track race," Olympian-turned-occasional commentator Shalane Flanagan, who won the 2017 New York Marathon, had said. The way he grinned as he pointed up to his left and then to his right was an expression of pure joy.

Kamworor broke through the tape in 2:08:13 and quickly made his way to the sideline, where his mentor, friend, and training partner

Kipchoge mirrored a wide smile as they embraced in a brotherly hug. Kipchoge can relate to that feeling of the finish line tape gracing across the chest, exclusive to just six men annually in the World Marathon Majors circuit.

On this occasion in 2019, Kamworor's second New York City Marathon title, he became $100,000 richer for winning, plus an extra $15,000 for running sub-2:09.

What if, on this fall Sunday, Kamworor had slipped on his Nikes, his race-ready footwear of choice, and stood on the starting line in Staten Island at 9 A.M. in the 41-degree air? Would his arms tingle with goose bumps? Would his heart rate pump faster from nerves that perhaps he wouldn't admit, not even to himself?

Twice a champion at the world's largest marathon, he wouldn't avoid being under a microscope by media, race organizers, sponsors, and those running fans who know how to correctly pronounce his name: KAMO-ROAR.

What if he could be in this race, a goal his mind adopted several months ago, while he was sitting alone on his stationary bike, repetitively pedaling, saving his joints from the pressure of experiencing two to three times his body weight if he ran?

Who among the men's elite pool, which also includes training partner Augustine Choge as well as Olympic marathon silver medalist Abdi Nageeye, could challenge him?

What if.

But Kamworor lives in the *now*, not the *what if.* And the now is a revised plan of competing in the Valencia Marathon in four Sundays on December 5. Valencia is the only option remaining for this year, he says. A 13.5-hour flight when the layover is slim, to challenge Geoffrey versus Geoffrey. It will be a much needed status update after a bumpy yearlong rebound from crutches to race contender. His participation was announced in the media in early October. "Set to lead Kenya's onslaught in Valencia," read a headline in Kenya's *The Star.*

While it's not the prestige of New York, the personal record–friendly course is an Elite Platinum Label Road Race. A mass participation marathon of roughly 23,000, it will include more than 120 men that have run 26.2 miles in less than 2:20. Kamworor's marathon personal best before the race in Valencia stands at 2:06:12, achieved at his debut in the distance in Berlin in 2012.

The experience in Spain's "city of running" won't compare to the wave of noise that flows along the New York City Marathon course. But never mind that, because regardless of the distance he runs, his ears ring silent when he's focused.

Passion for running. Must. Self-belief. Must. Determination. Must. That's what got him through another cycle of rehab.

In the now, Kamworor is healed, physically. His mileage has escalated upward of 30 kilometers a day: 20 in the morning and 10 in the evening, for the last six weeks, building up to the Valencia Marathon. Now, his mind has moved on. Or "grabbed a higher branch," as he'd say, in an echo of Sang's philosophy.

The day before the New York City Marathon, Kamworor was on his farm, a few miles from training camp, relaxing among cattle and sipping a cup of tea. An easy Saturday after his morning run before driving 15 miles to Eldoret to spend less than 48 hours with his wife and their five children, all under the age of eight.

The sun had already slipped undercover in Eldoret as Korir inches closer to the finish line a world away in New York. "I must focus to do great in Valencia," Kamworor's thought as he watches the live screen footage. And even though the house is calm, his mind continues to race. His two oldest sons point to the TV.

"Kwa nini haukimbii," they ask. *Why are you not running?*

"Two years ago I was in this race, and I won," he says. He shows them a photo of his 2019 marathon victory hanging on a wall in the house.

"In four weeks, I'll be running, and you'll be watching me on the TV."

UPTICK

A man toting a panga walks by at 6:06 A.M. as 37 runners and counting hover around Sang and his staff. The man must be on the way to a field somewhere with the African machete to cut vegetation. It's more usual to find a larger group; not all belong to the training camp. "Eighty percent of the people here we are helping," Sang will say for any given morning training session.

A trio of women are expectedly outnumbered; one is hearing impaired. Chepyego is here in a pink long-sleeved shirt, black tights, and fluorescent green socks to warm her slim body. Peter Nduhui, the camp's physiotherapist, masked under a white cap and a black jacket labeled with "Kenya" on the back, stands next to Kipchoge and the two Korirs. While it's not cold enough to see one's breath, one runner is resisting the nippy temperature by wrapping himself in a coat suitable for winter.

Veins protrude on chiseled calves bound for a 40-kilometer pilgrimage on tarmac perched above the escarpment. Thursdays are for long runs.

This is a test. This is only a test.

Kamworor will run half the distance as he tapers his volume in advance of the Valencia Marathon, his first marathon of 2021. He feels ripe for the occasion taking place in 10 days. Aiming to win. He later says it out loud in a tone that distinguishes confidence from consideration. "I'm good to go."

Appropriately named "the Boston route" for the stretch of long, rolling hills, the scenic loop around Kaptagat will absolutely steal one's breath, not simply because it propels the heart rate as they run upward of 2,700 meters (8,858 feet), but also because of the backdrop of the valley and a lush blanket of greenery and flora. While it's a beautiful gift for the eyes, it can feel like an orchestrated assault to the body—even at 60 percent effort, which for an elite like Korir is a reduced pace of 3:39 minutes per kilometer (a 5:52-minute mile, for nearly 25 miles).

In quick succession, the cluster of runners take off trotting not a second later than 6:23 A.M. The Toyota van pulls away from the camp's blue gate, leaving behind puffs of dirt as it begins to trace the route, first cutting onto the tarmac before pursuing a rocky dirt road between maize fields.

The morning is quiet, yet full of movement. Children walk to school, navigating around a string of cattle along the road. A man cycles with a steel canister full of milk attached to the back of his bicycle. It's a job that the guy running in an oversized white shirt and orange Nike shorts can relate to. In a parallel world, would that be Kipchoge, had circumstances been different?

The coin has two sides in life, he says.

Long before Kipchoge became a two-time Olympic marathon champion and world record holder, as a teenager he would bike up to 40 kilometers roundtrip a day around his hometown delivering fresh milk from his family's farm to a local market in exchange for roughly a dollar per liter of milk.

The story goes that one day his bike broke five kilometers from the milk depot. He ran to a friend's house to borrow another bike so he could proceed to deliver the perishable staple.

How ironic that Kipchoge is running by a guy that mirrors his former self. The shape of his life couldn't be more different—out here gracefully charging along, making a training run that nearly equals a marathon look deceptively easy. He is determined and in tune, affirmed by a fixed gaze as he strides along a rocky dirt path before transitioning onto the tarmac.

Training partners vouch that Kipchoge is never out of character. This is who he is, a man so diligent that he hasn't missed a training session, save for a business trip that pulls him out of the country. He has the same face wherever he is. Kipchoge's presence elevates the morale at camp, Sang says.

Innate wisdom perhaps, though layers have been added under the guidance of Sang. But what's the root of Sang's uncanny insight and intuition?

"I don't know," Sang says. He pauses. "That's who I am."

Two kilometers from the end of the run, Kipchoge and the others pick up the cadence. There's training pace, and then there's "Kipchoge pace." Only two others keep up—or rather, attempt to from behind. If Kipchoge is tired, sore, challenged, he doesn't wear it on his face or in his flawless form.

When he stops at 40 kilometers in Kaptagat, he flashes a smile. He slips into one of two support vehicles on site today. Apart from a comment that the route was challenging, he is mostly silent about the run and the topic of running. "I'm on page 15," he says of *A Promised Land*, Barack Obama's 768-page memoir.

MAKING HISTORY, TOGETHER

We all cried."

We as in old men. Old women. Mothers. Fathers. Young boys and girls. *We* as in anyone who was paying attention. Especially in Kenya.

"There was a big crowd in Eldoret. You put so many heads of Black people [together], it was like asphalt. The only difference is it was moving," Sang says, chuckling.

What was it about that moment, on October 12, 2019, in Vienna when Eliud Kipchoge defined himself and the sport as he proved possible what many thought wasn't—to run a marathon in less than two hours? That was a crying moment for the world, as Sang puts it.

Earlier that day, a Saturday, Sang went for a walk in the dark, misty morning. "Alone. I just wanted to be alone," he says. Sometimes he prefers to be that way. Likes keeping to himself in general. He says that he rarely speaks to the media, despite frequent interview requests. As one who is a self-described loner, he enjoys solitude. "I love staying alone. I have no problem. People think I'm crazy. On weekends when I'm not busy I stay at home. From Saturday until Monday. Read. Rest."

There are moments when Sang is not alone, yet he can feel alone. Ironically, those moments are when he's surrounded by people, like at camp. "Even when I'm with these people I feel alone. Besides what brings us together, what else is there?" he says.

Sang speaks about a close friend, originally from Kenya but who has Danish citizenship. "This guy," as he refers to him and not by name, he can sit with the whole day. Kindred spirits. A personal connection. Camp is different. Camp is less that and more "a vehicle for transmission," in Sang's words. A relationship limited to the service you provide. A professional connection.

As Sang continued to walk alone, his mind wandered. Not about the moment. He didn't want to think about the moment. Because "when you think about the moment, you get distracted." He thought about the situation. Like the weather, which was just shy of 50 degrees Fahrenheit.

Somewhere away from his walk alone in the dark, misty morning, the boy who once approached Sang for a training plan was counting down to the monumental endeavor he was about to embark on: the INEOS 1:59 Challenge, Kipchoge's second attempt to break the two-hour mark for a marathon.

And the boy who became a man the world was watching was ready.

So focused, Sang remembers. Imagine the impact. "Everything is on your shoulders. Everything. And you're the only one." Sang speaks about Kipchoge. "Sometimes you think, *Am I doing the right thing?*"

Yes, a real thought. "Of course, you don't tell anybody, and you don't want to show that you're not sure of yourself. The athlete can panic."

All along here was a guy who had a mind that surprised even Sang. "How do you quantify a strong mind?" He asks the question out loud in a way as though the air will respond.

"I think he was always like that," Sang reflects on Kipchoge's sense of focus. "I could see the guy had gone into another mode, an extra mode of activating his mental strength," Sang says of that day in Vienna.

Certain things activate your senses. "It's like always being on the road, and one day you decide to buy a car. But all along you've been seeing cars. The eyes are programmed in a certain way. Your eyes start seeing things. Your heart starts listening to things that it wasn't listening to before. And then the brain starts adjusting." Sang had always been aware of Kipchoge's mental acuity, but not in the context of being as powerful as what Kipchoge would display on this day.

"What is interesting of the mind about this guy, from the moment I started training him, he's never asked anything about training. Never. He comes to training for training."

When Kipchoge and Sang had first embarked on the journey to attempt to run a marathon in less than two hours in 2017, Nike's Breaking2 project, "there was so much negativity on social media when it was announced. 'It's impossible.' Some scientists were saying it will take another 75 years before a human being comes close," Sang recalls. "People are entitled to their opinions, so who am I to argue with their opinions."

"The power of blocking all of that negativity and focusing, it was unbelievable. If it was me, I would have been affected," Sang says.

He continues, "Truly we have not explored the human potential in whatever we do as far as the contribution of mental strength is concerned. That is an area I'm still trying to understand."

The event in Vienna was held 165 meters above sea level, making it opportune to run faster compared to being at high altitude, where the amount of oxygen is less available. The INEOS 1:59 Challenge involved a total of 41 pacers that were rotated in and out of the race and were instructed to run in V formation in front of Kipchoge for maximum aerodynamics. Two pacemakers also ran behind him. These men were instrumental in sweeping Kipchoge to the finish.[*]

---

[*]   Among the talent: Norwegian brothers Jakob, Filip, and Henrik Ingebrigtsen (all world-class middle-distance runners); Hillary Bor, a 3,000-meter steeplechase US champion (and US Army staff sergeant); Olympian Kota Murayama, who specializes in 5,000 and 10,000 meters (the lone Japanese pacemaker in the event); and Ugandan Jacob Kiplimo, who just a few years prior had competed in the Rio Olympics at 15 years old.

A smile had spread across Kipchoge's face as he sprinted with 200 meters remaining, pointing to both sides of the boisterous crowd. Sang was jumping up and down, flailing his arms above his head. This was the only time that he saw himself as being part of the race. There, at the finish line.

Kipchoge pounded his chest twice as he ran through the finish line in 1:59:40. The stunning and historic feat was described as a "moon landing moment"—a barrier-breaking achievement that few thought would happen in this generation, or ever. Notably, Kipchoge's INEOS 1:59 Challenge generated 4.9 million YouTube views and reached more than 500 million TV viewers at the time, according to Sunset+Vine, a UK television sports production and media company that was the host broadcaster of the event.

Due to the rotation of professional pacers and the fact that the race wasn't an open competition, Kipchoge's sub-two-hour effort isn't considered the official marathon world record. The time was a symbolic record that had proved something about humanity. As Kipchoge would say, "No human is limited." Still, Sang had led Kipchoge to the accomplishment, which he credited as much to Kipchoge's intellectual acumen as to his physical conditioning. "He confirmed to me that mental strength supersedes everything," Sang says.

"The best competitor is yourself," Kipchoge repeats the words that Coach taught him back in 2003. "Respect yourself, and when you are on a starting line, know that you are the best-trained person." You are your best competitor.

"The way he soaks in information, the way he internalizes, the way he executes it," Sang says. "It made me realize that as a human being, if you use your mind very well, what we normally achieve, we can achieve maybe 10 percent or even 20 percent more. All along I was teaching him, but here is a guy who is teaching me that the mind can supersede anything."

The boy who became a man the world was watching hugged Sang tightly, though briefly, as their embrace was quickly intercepted by several pacers, who hoisted Kipchoge above their heads as he toted the Kenyan flag.

"In my mind, I don't think I would be where I am without Patrick. I don't think I would run the way that I am running or perform well without him," Kipchoge says. Had Kipchoge been under a different coach, he doesn't trust that he would have made the transition to the marathon. He doesn't think he would have broken any marathon record either. "I'm really happy for the guidance. I'm happy for everything."

Kipchoge is at a loss for a singular word to describe what his coach continues to mean to him. "I've interacted with Patrick as far as life is concerned, as far as the sport is concerned, as far as business is concerned. When I actually put it in one cup—life, sport, and business—and try to mix them, I cannot get the right word to describe."

Eliud Kipchoge, a gift to the world, as he was called.

But Patrick Sang, too. The man who wrapped the gift.

mvumilivu hula mbivu

a patient man eats a ripe fruit

RACE READY

Geoffrey Kamworor boards a plane at Jomo Kenyatta International Airport in Nairobi bound for Europe on Tuesday, November 30, 2021. Thirteen hours in transit, stopping at Paris Charles de Gaulle en route to Valencia, Spain, where he will compete in the marathon after a two-year hiatus from the distance. A lengthy pilgrimage to run on crowdless pavement. The flight is the easy part.

Eight days ago, Kamworor celebrated his birthday. His mind is more aged than 29, always ready to cooperate with whatever the reality.

"You must accept," he says.

"Accept the way it has happened."

It as in a year and a half reboot. The solo run at dawn. The unaware motorbike driver. The knockout. Fractured leg. Emergency surgery. Stitches. Crutches. Scars. Flatlined athleticism. A peak of progress. Olympic Trials win. Fractured foot. Forfeited Olympics. Mending the ineffable heartbreak on a stationary bike, round after round to also heal physically.

Negativity did not shadow him. His mind is conditioned to peel away from the thought of *have not*. Even with just six weeks of preparation, he can and will race.

This is part of his push-pull fate, how he'll end the 2021 rollercoaster season: recovered from injury. *Finally*. Ready to race. *Finally*. Coach did not set a target. The expectation is to challenge himself, give his best. Not that Kamworor knows anything less.

Valencia is a city that has been good to Kamworor in years past. It's where he became a half marathon world champion in 2018. Perhaps here will mark his return to greatness.

Sunday, December 5, 2021. His feet are nimble, light as they push off warm asphalt. This morning in Valencia—referred to in Spanish as Ciudad del Running, the city of running—differs from his typical Sunday, when he would otherwise be at home in Eldoret, relaxing with his children and his wife. But his ordinary schedule is disrupted by a hard-fought and welcome agenda of finally competing in the marathon after his body has healed. The question is not can he measure up, but rather, how well will he?

Among the top-10 fastest entrants in the men's elite field is a minute detail. Today is the by-product of someone who trusted the process. Even though that process was distracted by setbacks. The surgery. The foot fracture. A missed Olympics. Physical roadblocks more than mental. There seems to be an ironclad arrangement with his mind, an unspoken vow. His inner consciousness sees the light. "I will do my best," he says six days before the race. Words that will stream in his consciousness in time leading up to this Sunday morning.

Kamworor showed up aiming for position over personal best as the objective. Sidelined no longer, the race is a cumulative test of his will. There's an objective down the road that Kamworor mentioned one day at camp. A marathon like Valencia will prepare him for a much bigger picture.

"I've been following in his footsteps," Kamworor says of Kipchoge. "I want to do more than what he has done in the marathon. That's what I can say."

"He always believes in what he does. He has always said, 'Everything is possible.'" Kamworor says that the two joke often. "I tell him,

'My friend, you break the records now. When I come fully into the marathon, I'll break your record.'"

"If you can break my record, it will be something nice," Kipchoge responded.

Something nice.

Call it something grand to attempt a pilgrimage that traces Kipchoge's footsteps. But someone has to be groomed to go for it. That someone must be consistent in his performances. That someone must free his mind of mental roadblocks. Show up to training without questioning. Show up to races without questioning.

In Valencia, Kamworor proves he is consistent. His pace fluctuates little: 4:48, 4:46, 4:48, 4:48, 4:49, 4:49, 4:49, 4:48, 4:49. The pattern brings him to the finish line in 2:05:23—11 seconds behind winner Lawrence Cherono of Kenya. The fourth-place mark in the race was also Kamworor's lifetime best in the distance.

"I'm happy for him," Sang says. "He has matured. He knows himself."

One step at a time, Kamworor continues to dare himself, and he delivers. "I have many goals in life," he says. "When the right time comes."

REVESTING

Mid-December somewhere in the Maasai Mara National Reserve in southwest Kenya, an elephant stands in a stream, trunk pulling leaves from a branch overhead. His existence here is proof that life is welcome, though much of the surrounding 580-square mile domain in Kenya could suggest otherwise. A prolonged drought has turned the savanna a depleted hue—brown and crunchy grassland decorated with strips of cracked mud, some of which would be pockets of water if circumstances were different.

One safari guide insists that this part of the Serengeti, commonly referred to as "the Mara," usually doesn't appear so withered and depressed. Normally, the land receives 3.4 inches of rainfall monthly. But the guide estimates that rain hasn't greeted the game-studded reserve in roughly 12 weeks and counting.

The terrain is usually more romantic—fields of tall green grasslands and saturated streams, an idyllic haven for the "Big Five" (lions, elephants, buffaloes, leopards, and rhinos) and the "Big Nine," which adds giraffes, cheetahs, hippos, and zebras. Their lives, part of nearly 90 species of mammals here, are a reason why the Mara attracts thousands of international visitors annually.

If harsh weather conditions continue, so does concern from conservationists, who point out that suppressed rains can disrupt life considerably. For example, Africa's Great Wildebeest Migration, when roughly 1.5 million wildebeest, accompanied by hundreds of thousands of zebras, gazelles, and an array of other wildlife, roam hundreds or sometimes even two-thousand miles roundtrip across the vast plains of the Serengeti in Tanzania northward to Maasai Mara in Kenya. The journey is a struggle for survival, vulnerable to predatory lions and cheetahs as well as the Nile crocodile–infested Grumeti and Mara Rivers.

The annual migration, beginning in the spring, is considered to be one of the greatest wildlife spectacles on the planet. The pounding of hooves in search of greener pastures is dictated by weather patterns. But the rains continue to be unpredictable, not just here, but across the country. It is particularly detrimental to the farmland.

"Climate change is real," Sang repeatedly says. "It's hotter, and it's going to get worse. Most of the injuries we got in 2019, we had a lot of rain. Lots of rain, from 2018 onward."

Sang's athletes understand the message the environment around them is sending, Kipchoge on a more visible level. He knows that education is a key to helping Kenyans adapt to the changing climate. In September 2021, he officially established the Eliud Kipchoge Foundation with two primary goals: to protect the environment and to assist with education programs in Kenya and eventually across borders.

An avid reader since childhood, Kipchoge is adamant about giving youth more access to books, which he believes are powerful tools that can help improve communities. His voice lifts when he talks about his aim to build libraries across the country—and all over the world—in all schools so children can hopefully develop an appreciation for education, he says.

"I trust one day things will come, and we will build libraries in the whole country." He continues. "After finishing in Kenya, I want to go to Uganda. Rwanda, DRC. We need to get those kids from mining areas, get them to go to school. That's the only way to bring development."

Learning is ageless. "There is no winner of education," Kipchoge says. "Think in an infinite way." He points to its value in sport, saying it's necessary for well-rounded development. There is a distinguishable difference between an amateur and a professional, Kipchoge explains. That includes how he uses his mind. One can be blessed with the best talent in the world, but that doesn't necessarily classify him as a professional.

"Even in the Olympics or World Championships, you can get two world champions or two Olympic gold medalists. One might be an amateur, and one might be a professional. An amateur is that person . . . if there's training at 4 p.m., he can rush to town and do other things. That's a real amateur. A real professional is one who is treating everything that he's doing in a professional way," Kipchoge explains.

"If you have education, and you marry education and talent, you can go far. You can propel that talent," Kipchoge says. "Part of being a professional is conditioning your mind through education. If you lack education, there is no way you can be a professional. No way."

As for the environment, Kipchoge adopted 50 hectares of Kaptagat Forest in June 2020. "I believe together we can make dry land green again, which has a huge impact on biodiversity, water availability, and healthy food," he states on his foundation's website. His motive is to plant more trees and to make full use of farms. "Without forests, you cannot breathe." Part of his first stage of projects with the foundation is to plant a forest in all 47 counties of Kenya.

"Only indigenous trees," he says. "They grow slowly. Nobody is interested in indigenous trees as far as getting the timber. It will take more than 50 years [for the trees to grow]. It's a way to conserve the environment," Kipchoge explains.

He is starting in Kaptagat and hopes to convince each county to conserve a portion of forest, fence it, and plant trees. He hopes to spread the idea around East Africa, then across the continent.

Advocating for environmental conservation, at the beginning of November 2021, Kipchoge attended the United Nations Climate Change Conference in Glasgow, Scotland, where more than 100 world leaders pledged to reduce the impact of climate change. That included declaring to end and reverse deforestation by 2030. Kipchoge, alongside President Kenyatta, spoke on behalf of Kenya, representing Africa's voice on the climate crisis.

President Kenyatta delivered Kenya's national statement, explaining that "In Kenya, extreme weather events, including floods and droughts, lead to losses of between 3 to 5 percent of our GDP annually. Further, they aggravate food insecurity and trigger divisive intra-community and inter-country competition for resources."

Kenya is centered on the equator, and the country experiences its seasons in periods of long and short rains. Climate change is making such periods increasingly unpredictable. The rainy seasons either "hardly bring any water, and sometimes they flood our farm fields, ruining all the crops," Kipchoge said during his nearly five-minute speech.

"There are Western countries who are so advanced in data and innovation but who have futile moves from that initial feeling for the climate whereby in Africa we feel so closely," Kipchoge said, urging Western leaders to work with Africa to address climate change.

Kipchoge, the human being, leading by example, just like Kipchoge the athlete.

As Sang would explain, Kipchoge is self-aware. When everybody is looking up to you, you become a role model, and "if you don't internalize, then you don't know who you are. Then you will be seeing the sport in a narrow way," Sang says. "Running is only a small part of life. You still have so many other things that are related to human life, not directly linked to running."

Student of life first, athlete second. That's the actual journey.

A wordless chorus of feet stampede across the ground four days out from Christmas Day. More than three dozen athletes offer their long, lean muscles for the morning's calling: 2,000 meters, five times, followed by 1,000 meters, five times.

Wycliffe Kinyamal's brawny quads are masked in tight black shorts. As his muscles hammer through the early reps, his lungs dance with the thin air, leaving his mouth ajar. A look of someone trying. To be out here is to engage in a necessary struggle, Coach says. That's a building block to rise to the top.

Nearly blinkless eyes dig into their respective palace of goals as they train. Some faces are stamped with gritted expressions, as though their will is being physically scrimmaged and they are bent on winning the game.

Sang's white Nike cap shields his head against the wind slapping all around. It smacks the trees and brushes loose dirt into the air. The usual sun hides behind a curtain of gray clouds. Warmth will not enter this day, the shortest of the year, and a layer is a must at the moment. "This is winter," Sang jokes. Technically today marks the official beginning of astronomical winter in the Northern Hemisphere, a return of more sunlight.

When will the pace of life ever calm down? Sang is still here. He is still going, though he admits that because of his age, he would like to slow down a little bit. "Being responsible takes a lot of energy," he says, laughing deep from the belly.

Coach chuckles during some training sessions. The endearing echo can be heard from halfway across the field. From the same distance, Kipchoge is packaged within a string of 30-plus men lapping in lane 1. He blends in just as much as he stands out. Wide bouncy stride, steady and tireless posture, as though he runs to demonstrate tangible perfection. Kipchoge scurries past an empty plastic bottle strung on a stick marking 200 meters. The group he's sandwiched in is like a sort of running peloton, each athlete respectfully spaced.

Jackline Chepkoech is among the cable of athletes grouped into separate paces. Hers is a more independent exertion. Becoming more experienced, her running is blossoming. Four months ago, on August 20 in Nairobi, Chepkoech raced mostly solo in the women's 3,000-meter steeplechase at the Moi International Sports Centre during the World Athletics Under-20 Championships. Just as she had done at races leading into this one, Chepkoech set herself apart from the competition by spreading a 30-meter lead on the first of seven and a half laps. The effort escorted her to a gold medal and a personal record, 9:27.40. It was a hard-earned victory after Chepkoech competed in the Olympic Trials, finishing fourth and narrowly missing a spot on Kenya's team bound for Tokyo. She erupted in excitement, making an immediate victory lap. Sang has coined her a nickname: "Champion."

The Champion projects competing in senior races in 2022, including the Commonwealth Games in Birmingham, England, a springboard to other prominent international competitions. Like every athlete here today, she understands the exchange needed to continue to elevate herself. What will become of her restless drive?

"Remember that opportunities come once," Selly Chepyego later addresses the entire camp post-training during an hour-and-a-half meeting that promptly begins at 11 A.M., exactly one hour and 44 minutes after the athletes trickled off the track. "We are lucky here."

The assembly begins with a prayer from Chepyego as coaches and athletes stand from their circle of white plastic chairs:

"Tunashukuru mungu kwa huu mwaka ambao tumepata mafanikio. Pia tunapoanza mkutano hii mungu utupe maarifa na utuongoze. Naomba haya katika jina la yesu kristo, aminina."

As we usher in another year, we thank God for this successful year. As we begin this meeting, may God grant us wisdom and guide us. I ask this in the name of Jesus Christ.

A notebook lay open on Kipchoge's lap as his hands fiddle with a blue pen. His mouth and nose are sheltered by a blue face mask as he listens carefully to physiotherapist Peter Nduhui, who continues the meeting by addressing concerns about COVID-19 and the uncertainty surrounding a new variant, Omicron. With the two-week holiday break about to commence, it is more important than ever to practice responsible measures, he reminds the group. Social distance. If you feel any symptoms, seek a medical professional. Nduhui transitions to directives about minding the body, that the mattress one sleeps on can affect your back. Take care of your running gear, too, he says. Worn-out shoes can affect performance. The athletes nod, absorbing his words in agreement.

Sang continues 30 minutes into the meeting, taking the center of the circle. "I mind my own security," he begins. Sang has noticed strangers coming to training sessions. He wants to contain the group. A number of athletes at camp sponsor and support unmanaged talent who live nearby. Come January 4, 2022, the coaching staff should be informed as to which athletes outside of official management should be training with the group, good people, Sang clarifies.

He carries on about whereabouts information and the Registered Testing Pool managed by the World Anti-Doping Association, requiring a selection of elites to frequently specify their location and contact information to Anti-Doping Organizations.

Sadly, the dangerous lure of performance enhancing drugs has become inevitable in modern sports. From swimming to road cycling and Major League Baseball, the temptation to dope is something that athletes must try to avoid as they fight to make their name and increase their value in sports. Elite marathoners and track athletes are no exceptions.

As Kenya's athletics reputation has increasingly come under fire, Sang's attention deepens. Developing the whole person as well as his emphasis on community at training camp is his way of helping athletes resist the influence of those who might encourage doping.

"Somebody can qualify and miss championships. When you are in the Whereabouts, I think the best thing is to make sure you follow those things because those guys can victimize you," Sang says. Once, a member of the Athletics Integrity Unit called Sang at midnight about a certain athlete. Sang wasn't aware his name was used as a reference. "From January, we want to be a smaller team. People we know," Sang says. "We need to be closer so that I know you have listed me."

"Morally, you don't want to leave them," he says of the influx of outsiders that have continued to attend his respected workouts. But at the same time, "when you have a smaller group, you give better service," he points out.

Chepkoech listens quietly. A pink bracelet labeled "Eliud Kipchoge Foundation" peeks from her left wrist as she sits, hands folded across her lap. A fly crawls over her toes, the nails of which offer evidence of someone overly dedicated to the sport. Their rough, short, and scratched surface has never received a pedicure.

A round of words are shared from a few athletes, including Laban Korir. Kinyamal closes the meeting by leading a rhythmic Maasai clap. He demonstrates the cadence. *Clap . . . clap-clap.* The group follows his directive. *Clap . . . clap-clap.* One. *Clap . . . clap-clap.* Two. *Clap . . . clap-clap.* Three. *Clap. Clap-clap.* Four.

At 12:30 P.M., they break for lunch of rice and beans. Simple, wholesome, nourishing.

Life at camp.

IN THE LONG RUN

I was in Taipei," Sang begins a once-upon-a-time story, reflecting on a memorable morning run during which he witnessed a large group of people exercising together in a plaza. Later, a thought struck him that should he ever move away from his home country, he'd want to be in a particular environment such as that, one in which people come together with the intention to practice something healthy. It's a mindset as much as it is a way of life. "Imagine if I was living in a place where we have hundreds of people like that," he says. "That positive energy will be amazing. People who exercise a lot don't have time for negative things."

There will be another way to live after coaching, perhaps a world in which Sang doesn't run alone in the afternoon. What is the afterlife to this current chapter? Sang doesn't know yet, though he laughingly verbalizes one truth: "I want to experience life differently," he says. "I'd rather be responsible for myself."

Perhaps life will involve world travels. South America is on his list of places to visit, as are Botswana and Rwanda, the latter of which he says would be a learning experience. "I'm really intrigued by their vision," Sang says. "Their vision is driven by something called ubuntu. Unity of purpose, caring for one another. It's a very rich human value."

For now, Sang will continue to influence and enrich the lives of his athletes. While he is no longer under Olympic pressure, his schedule has yet to clear. There are goals on the line, dreams to fulfill, more athletes to develop—to be stronger, to be faster, to learn how to endure. To be honest. To be disciplined. To be responsible. To be mindful.

And in the midst of learning how to become a better runner, one also learns how to become a better person.

Marathoner Selly Chepyego echoes a shared sentiment about what living and training at camp has taught her about approaching life. "Everything that you do in your life, go for it," she says simply. It's all possible.

These are words to hold close when the time comes to face a hard reality: an athlete's career will eventually end. When an athlete must pivot, what does life outside of running look like when they can no longer keep up? Some speak of getting into business endeavors. Chepyego thinks about segueing into coaching. Kipchoge would consider it a "side dish" to the main endeavor he envisions in his future: going around the world to inspire youth and encourage others to make running a lifestyle. He hopes to do more of that through his foundation.

"When you inspire somebody," Kipchoge says, "that's the happiest moment. When you have touched somebody's heart, changed somebody's life, even the way he's thinking. That's the best thing."

Dewdrops seem to have touched every blade of grass by the time Victor Chumo steps onto the tarmac at 6:11 A.M. Portions of the road have been stamped with a thin layer of sticky mud left behind by tires after the night served a torrential downpour. These days the rain has been less predictable. Sang has to plan ahead.

"How we design a training program may change a little bit," Sang adds. "The times running on a dirt road and running on the tarmac, they are not the same. When you are monitoring performance, you also have to be conscious of the fact that you are not running so much on soft ground. Soft ground takes energy."

Chumo, dressed in skin-tight black shorts and a black long-sleeve layered under a white T-shirt, is ready to embrace 30K out-and-back one early Thursday morning. The directive is "easy pace," which for him translates to 4 minutes per kilometer (approximately 6:26-minute miles). "I enjoy that," he says. "No pressure."

Chumo takes off, a particle among three dozen guys. Each one is out here adding another layer of endurance and mental consistency to the sum of his parts, their currents intersecting into a cohesive heartbeat on the road. There is no music or chatter to distract from the workout's physical and psychological lesson, just the ebb and flow of lungs catching air and feet hitting the ground.

The workout is a lesson in sensory mindfulness. Chumo feels the smooth evenness of the tarmac as his lungs inhale and exhale. He silently tells himself to keep persevering. Day in, day out. Keep persevering. This is how he'll reach a particularly precious goal—to compete in his first marathon, which is a stepping stone to a destination architected in his mind. In another tomorrow, he wants to compete in the New York City Marathon. "Compete" is light wording. He wants to win—and, yes, he says it out loud.

In another future, Chumo is already thinking about life after running. He speaks of wanting to stay involved in the sport, serving as a commentator in addition to getting into motivational speaking. He is drawn to books about famous speeches, like *100 World's Greatest Speeches*, which he reads during his downtime. This life is in contrast to what he had in mind growing up. Chumo wanted to become a tour guide in Kenya; he wanted to learn several European languages. That plan changed the more he grew into running. He felt obliged to take another path when he decided to take running to another level.

The sky's blanket of stars has cleared and reformed into an unstained azure. The sun is suspended behind Chumo as he runs on a mostly vacant road in Kaptagat toward Eldoret. It looks as though he is chasing his outstretched shadow. In a sense, he is, the silhouette symbolic of the faster version of himself. The one that wants to debut in the marathon in 2:05.

A truth is ahead of him in the form of a 5-foot-6, 125-pound mentor, whose bouncy stride looks as though he's oversaturated with energy. The only guy in a white Nike cap blends into the cluster. Kipchoge's fluorescent knee-high socks wrap his chiseled legs. He is focusing on the pace and on the road. *Are we on the target? Is the energy still okay?* His thoughts are in the moment. But once in a while, Kipchoge's mind will wander into other things.

"When I'm running, I get a lot of ideas," Kipchoge says. Sometimes those ideas relate to his shoes and apparel. Other occasions, he thinks about the grandness of running, the accessibility. One day, Kipchoge wants to make one of his ideas a reality: "to get people to run at the same time everywhere around the world. Everything can stop and we run."

"Run as one" is what Kipchoge voices. "Use running to bring people together in a peaceful way. We need to think together. All of us are from a human family." The only difference is the color of one's skin, he says. "We need to come to the table. Take care of this planet. If you run as one, you think together, bring development together. That's how to enjoy life."

Yes, running has the power to do that, Kipchoge says.

Sang's eyes peer out of the support car window, which is covered in condensation from the cold morning. He observes Kipchoge's effort, as do children in green school uniforms, who stand on the side of the road in silence, their chestnut brown eyes awestruck. Do they recognize the sport's king? Or are they simply mesmerized by the hypnotic rhythm of his strides?

A moment of déjà vu. The children observe Kipchoge, just as Kipchoge as a child had watched Sang.

AFTERWORD

Each day awakens Kaptagat with a unique brightness. As the sun begins to reveal itself to the world, dozens of feet touch the earth with purpose. Under a soft glow of morning light, figures that appear more ethereal than real quietly go to work, swiftly tagging the ground with footprints. Their dedication is unspoken, rather illustrated by a pure and disciplined way of life, under the same roof, powered and empowered by togetherness.

During my time in Kenya, I encountered the Swahili phrase *tunagawana jua*, which translates to "we share the sun," the inspiration for the title of this book.

This shared source of light carries a particular weight and is exceptionally respected in various cultures around the world, including in Kenya. The country's Kalenjin community traditionally worshiped the sun, a supreme deity referred to as Asis.

The power of the sun provides life-giving energy needed for survival for all ecosystems and is what makes Acacia grow.

The national tree of Kenya, which is illustrated on the cover, also has significance. Acacia, "the best tree," as Kipchoge once told me, is able to survive in tough conditions. The Acacia's remarkable resilience is symbolic of perseverance—qualities that Sang and his athletes embody.

ACKNOWLEDGMENTS

The truth about writing a book is that it is an exceptional privilege that also carries great responsibility. The process has repeatedly tested my discipline and courage. While *We Share the Sun* is a singular project, writing it was a culmination of everything I've learned about storytelling. It's a dream destined since childhood and brought to life by many people who gave me a chance to go this route.

My love for writing started as a child, when my mother constantly fed me books and frequently toted me along to the local library. I naturally drifted to the sports section, unknowingly conditioning my mind for a future career in sports media. My passion for reading quickly transpired into writing. I'm grateful that I understood my direction at an early age and that I had wonderful role models.

I thank many people for their encouragement, firstly my grandmother Ginny, whose generosity, selfless principles, and open-mindedness has taught me necessary morals and a genuine way to live.

Karen Gerboth, my first editor in college, who took a chance on hiring a persistent junior student as a writing intern. Your influence continues to affect me, sixteen years later (and counting).

The editors that helped shape my development after I became a professional, a journey that started with Rachel Trem, who brought me onto her editing team when I was fresh out of college. I'm grateful to have worked alongside such an assertive and poised woman.

Ben Sylvan, who helped continue my writing journey, which brought me to New York City in 2011. And to Derek Samson, my former editor, now mentor who always understood my ability and has been essential in helping me bring my writing to life.

This book would not be possible without Jessica Case, who saw the vision and believed in me without question. I am blessed that our paths collided and that you allowed me to express my writing in a way that I've always wanted. I'm also grateful for the team at Pegasus Books that treated my manuscript with great care.

A very special thank you to Michael Petrik, an incredible person and mentor who has known me for nearly half of my life. I appreciate you being alongside me throughout the writing process. Thank you for your willingness to simply be there and for your honesty, constructive feedback, pep talks and for the beautiful discussions about writing, running, and life.

Eddy Cramm, a friend like you is a gift to my life.

Wan Man, one of the most solid and loyal people I've ever met. I am especially grateful for your support and enthusiasm throughout the project. Thank you for being you.

To Emo Rugene, thank you for your time, your spirit, your encouragement.

Amanda Hudson, you have an incredibly beautiful eye, and I thank you for the exceptional design of the book cover.

There were many individuals in Kenya whom I'm especially grateful for. Albert Kibet, the man who drove me between Iten and Kaptagat as early as 5 A.M. I appreciate that you always looked out for me and for our thoughtful conversations. To the people who lived parts of the journey alongside me in Kenya, your encouragement always made me smile: Hendrik Pfeiffer, Simon Kohler, Julian Alonso, Marcela Joglova, Marije Geurtsen. Thanks to Hugo van den Broek and Hilda Kibet of

Iten Accomodation, a very special place to write from. Carolyne Jep-kosgei and Chris de Lie, C&C feels like home away from home. Thank you for welcoming me. Caroline Kibet, you inspire me in ways I can't put into words. Brother Colm O'Connell, anyone should be so lucky to meet you. Thank you for your care and for making me laugh. A lot.

Much gratitude to my inner circle of women that inspire me: Rachel Wang, Nadin Duit, Lieve Leijssen, Rebekah Madebach, Megan McCormick, Alea James, Sofia Hedström de Leo, Melanie Sullivan, Anna Marshall, Mariana Salem, Ines Marquardt, Lindsay Novis, Miya Signor, Sara Little, Petra Krause, Caitlin Boston, Anna Freyman, and Nailya Bikmurzina.

And other friends who've supported the journey in some way: Nacho Valle, Rune Revsbæk, Réamonn Byrne, Tobias Singer, Josh Staph, and Jack Staph. Daniel Bach, I appreciate our friendship and for your encouragement. Nick Barili, you are an amazing person, and I'm grateful for the uplifting talks as I navigated the last phase of the editing process.

Thank you to Justin Brouckaert for your push and critical thinking early in the process and for helping to turn my ideas into something real.

Michel Boeting, thank you for our conversation.

To the incredibly inspiring athletes and people that offered their time and words, especially Eliud Kipchoge, Geoffrey Kamworor, Faith Kipyegon, Victor Chumo, Laban Korir, and Jonathan Korir. And the rest of the athletes at Global Sports Communication training camp, thank you for welcoming me. Thank you Jos Hermens for your time—and for your enthusiasm!

Most of all, thank you to Patrick Sang. I am grateful that you opened the door, for your trust, for your wisdom, and for your time. Thank you for being a positive and powerful light in this world.